WHAT IS THE GOSPEL ACCORDING TO PAUL?

JUSTIFICATION BY FAITH—God has provided a righteousness based not on what man can do but upon what He did in sending His Son as a sacrifice for sin.

JUSTIFICATION is not the reward for human striving but the free gift of God for those who will accept it by faith.

THEMES FROM ROMANS deals with JUSTIFICATION BY FAITH and its implications for Christian living.

THEMES FROM ROMANS

Robert H. Mounce

A Division of G/L Publications
Ventura, CA U.S.A.

The translation of all Regal books is under the direction of GLINT. GLINT provides technical help for the adaptation, translation and publishing of books for millions of people worldwide. For information regarding translation contact: GLINT, P.O. Box 6688, Ventura, California 93006.

2nd Printing, 1983

Scripture quotations in the publication are primarily from the *NIV—New International Version*, Holy Bible Copyright © 1978 by New York International Bible Society. Other versions, in alphabetical order, include:

AMP—AMPLIFIED BIBLE, The. Copyright © 1962, 1964 by Zondervan Publishing House. Used by permission.

Beck—The New Testament in the Language of Today by William F. Beck. Copyright © 1963 by Concordia Publishing House.

Conybeare, The Epistles of Paul by W. J. Conybeare, Baker Book House.

Goodspeed—The New Testament: An American Translation by Edgar J. Goodspeed. Copyright © 1923, 1948 by the University of Chicago.

JB, Jerusalem Bible, Copyright © 1966, 1967 and 1968 by Darton, Longman & Todd Ltd. and Doubleday and Company, Inc.

KJV—The Authorized King James Version.

Knox—The New Testament in the Translation of Monsignor Ronald Knox, Copyright © 1944 by Sheed and Ward, Inc., New York, with the kind permission of his Eminence, the Cardinal Archbishop of Westminster, and Burns and Oates, Ltd.

Lamsa, The Holy Bible from Eastern Manuscripts by George M. Lamsa. Copyright © 1940, 1957, 1961 by A. J. Holman Company.

Moffatt—The New Testament: A New Translation by James Moffatt, Copyright © 1964 by James Moffatt. Used by permission of Harper and Row, Inc., and Hodder and Stoughton, Ltd.

Montgomery—The Centenary Translation: The New Testament in Modern English translated by Helen Harrett Montgomery. Copyright © 1924, 1952 by the American Baptist Board of Education and Publication.

NEB—The New English Bible. © The Delegates of the Oxford University Press and The SYndics of the Cambridge University Press 1961, 1970. Reprinted by permission.

Phillips—THE NEW TESTAMENT IN MODERN ENGLISH, Revised Edition. J. B. Phillips, Translator. © J. B. Phillips 1958, 1960, 1972. Used by permission of Macmillan Publishing Co., Inc.

RSV—The Revised Standard Version of the Bible, copyrighted 1946 and 1952 by the Division of Christian Education of the NCCC, U.S.A., and used by permission.

TLB—The Living Bible by Kenneth N. Taylor, copyright © 1962, 1966 by Tyndale House Publishers.

TCNT—The Twentieth Century New Testament, Moody Bible Institute.

Weymouth—The New Testament in Modern English by Richard Francis Weymouth, as revised by J. A. Robertson. Reprinted by permission of Harper and Row Publishers, Inc., and James Clarke and Company Ltd.

Williams—The New Testament: A Translation in the Language of the People by Charles B. Williams. Copyright © 1937 by Bruce Humphries, Inc. Copyright renewed in 1965 by Edith S. Williams.

Library of Congress Cataloging in Publication Data
Mounce, Robert H.
  Themes from Romans.
  Bibliography: p.
  I. Bible. N.T.   Romans—Commentaries.   I. Title.
BS2665.3.M63   227'.106   81-51739
ISBN 0-8307-0774-3 (pbk.)   AACR2

Contents

A Teacher's Manual and Student Discovery Guides for Bible study groups using this book are available from your church supplier.

Introduction

Paul's letter to the church at Rome (written from Corinth during the winter months of A.D. 56 or 57) has had a major influence on the history of the Christian church. Its message has shaped and directed the thinking of such prominent leaders as Augustine, Calvin and Wesley. Luther called Romans "the chief book of the New Testament and the purest gospel." It is undoubtedly the finest expression of the Christian gospel.

How did it all begin?

Paul had just finished some three years of ministry in the Asian city of Ephesus. His plan was to visit Jerusalem via Macedonia and then press on to Rome (see Acts 19:21). Arriving in Greece he waited there for the winter months to pass (see Acts 20:3). It was during this period that he wrote his famous letter. The place of writing was probably Corinth (or its port city of Cenchrea). In support of this, note that at the end of the letter Paul mentions that he has been enjoying the hospitality of the house of Gaius (see Rom. 16:23) apparently the same Gaius that was converted at Corinth (see 1 Cor. 1:14). Consider also that Phoebe, who carried the letter to Rome, was a deaconess in the church in Cenchrea.

Paul's plans are rather clearly laid out in Romans 15:23-32. He had finished his work in the east and for years had longed to visit the believers in Rome. This he now plans to do on his way to Spain (see vv. 23,24). Paul had never been to Rome (see Rom. 1:10) although it had often been his intention (see Rom. 1:13; 15:22). In Paul's day the city of Rome boasted a population of over one million. It included an estimated 40 to 60 thousand Jews. According to the second century historian Tacitus, the Christians at Rome constituted "an immense multitude."

Where did this large group of believers come from? Some credit the church at Rome to the labors of Peter but this is highly unlikely. Peter appears to have been in Palestine until the time of the Apostolic Council (see Gal. 2:1-10), about A.D. 50. In Romans 16 Paul sends greetings by name to 26 friends in Rome—and Peter is not among them. Furthermore it was not Paul's practice to build on the foundations of others (see Rom. 15:20). The most likely suggestion is that the church had its start from travelers who had been converted to the Christian faith and returned to the capital city to share with others what they had learned.

One task remains before Paul can go to Rome. He must first go to Jerusalem accompanied by representatives of the churches in Macedonia and Achaia in order to deliver a contribution to the poor among the saints there (see Rom. 15:25-27). Paul anticipates trouble from the unbelievers in Judea and asks for prayer that he might be rescued from impending danger (see Rom. 15:30,31). His safe arrival at Rome—a time of joy and refreshment (see Rom. 15:32)—depends on it.

But let's go back to Corinth. Why did Paul write to the church at Rome? From the opening paragraphs of his letter it is clear that he longed to see them so that they might be "mutually encouraged by each other's faith" (Rom. 1:12). He says he was eager to preach the gospel to those at Rome (Rom. 1:15). However he had another agenda in mind as well. In chapter 15 he tells about his plan to visit them on his way to Spain (v. 24). In addition to enjoying their company he hopes they will assist him on his journey there. As he looks forward to evangelizing Spain he hopes that Rome will become to him in the west what Antioch was in the east.

From previous experience Paul knows that his enemies are skilled in twisting his message; Galatians is proof of that. So important are his plans for taking the gospel to the far reaches of the western empire that he cannot afford to have his message jeopardized in the very place which he intends to use as a base of operations. So he writes a rather full and complete presentation of the message he has been preaching. His purpose is to set forth in a logical way the doctrine of justification by faith and its implications for Christian living. His goal is to keep the gospel free from legalism without falling into the trap of antinomianism (conduct unrestrained by law).

One school of thought holds that Paul's basic purpose was to reconcile Jewish and Gentile elements in the church. While that was certainly a concern (note Romans 14 and 15:1-15) it was by no means the central purpose of the book. Nor should Romans be considered as the apostle's "last will and testament"—as if he were convinced that he would never make it to Rome. Romans is a magnificent presentation of the gospel—the good news that God has provided a righteousness based not on what man can do but upon what God did in sending His Son a sacrifice for sin. Man's responsibility is to respond in faith. Justification is not the reward for human striving but the free gift of God for those who will accept it by faith.

Please note that the book you are reading is not a

commentary in the usual sense of the word. It deals with specific topics and/or sections of Romans as they appear consecutively throughout Paul's letter. Thus, chapter 1 is a discussion of only three verses (1:18-20) while chapter 9 covers more than three chapters. We are concerned with the highlights of Romans. Because Paul wrote his letter in an orderly fashion the topics follow one another in such a way as to cover the entire subject of justification by faith and its implications for practical Christian living. The fact that portions of Romans are not covered in this approach does not detract from the apostle's basic presentation of the theme.

1

What Everyone Knows About God

Romans 1:18-20

The Bible never bothers to prove the existence of God; this is everywhere taken for granted. Anthropologists confess that they are unable to find a tribe of people anywhere in the world who do not worship some sort of divine being. No matter how remote the area or how ancient the tribe the evidences of mankind's religious longings are found everywhere. In India the temples of Hinduism dominate the landscape. Seek out an aboriginal tribe in the mountains of Peru and you will discover the centrality of the witch doctor and his sacred charms. Drive through rural America and see the churches that dot the countryside.

Historically people have spent little or no time arguing the existence of divinity. Of course, there are a few atheists, but atheism is not a natural state. It must be learned. It would never occur to the average person that the complexity of the universe and the unbelievable intricacies of the human body could be held to be the result of chance.

People cannot accept the presence of design without the prior existence of a Designer. Without a Creator there is no other option except the candid admission that what is—that is, matter itself—has always been. But the very idea of the eternality of matter boggles the mind. It simply will not do to reason that matter has *always* been—not just for a long time, but forever! Unless what is was created then it had no beginning. It won't do to evade the issue by saying we don't know how that could be. Our minds demand some larger orientation. The most reasonable starting point is God. Obviously, we don't know *how* He created *ex nihilo* (out of nothing), but we are pressed to the conclusion that He did. There is no acceptable alternative to the existence of a Creator-God.

Have you ever thought about how much faith it takes to be an atheist? In addition to denying the persuasiveness of such philosophical arguments as the argument from design (which in and of itself does not *prove* God's existence), the atheist must also believe that almost every person who ever lived was dead wrong about the one thing which was at the center of his existence. Not believing in God requires a lot more faith than believing in God!

In Romans 1:19,20 we learn that "what may be known about God is plain to them [that is, to "men who suppress the truth," v. 18], because God has made it plain to them." We also learn that "God's invisible qualities . . . have been clearly seen, being understood from what has been made." Note that this passage does not argue the existence of God. It does not set forth what theologians call a natural theology. It tells us, rather, that the God who created that which exists is a certain kind of God. He is a God who exercises wrath against those who suppress the truth. This wrath is not capricious but fair and just. Why? Because mankind is without excuse. God has revealed to everyone by means of the creation His essential nature. They are therefore "without excuse."

So as we study "What Everyone Knows About God," remember that we are assuming God's existence. That is why we titled the chapter, "What Everyone Knows. . . ."

What we want to learn is exactly what is commonly and universally known about God. What does creation reveal about the One who is behind everything that exists? Since man himself is so widely diverse in his cultural and technological settings, this common knowledge of God is bound to be basic. It pervades the consciousness of all men—modern sophisticate and ancient tribesman. This knowledge of God is basic to every man regardless of his culture, his place in history, or his degree of technological advancement.

The essential question, then, is moral. Since every man knows the fundamental truths about the nature of his Creator and these truths have definite ethical implications, it follows that he is by virtue of this knowledge responsible to respond in a certain way. Verses 21 through 32 in Romans 1 describe the downward spiral of man in his refusal to accept what he knows to be true. If man were left in the dark about the nature of God and what this implies from an ethical standpoint, he would not be responsible for his conduct. Without God (an absolute) there would be no right or wrong. But the point is that man *does* know God and therefore must bear full responsibility for his sinful actions.

No one is excluded. No one can get away with saying, "I don't believe in God." As someone said, "You can't turn out the light by closing your eyes." The heathen who has never heard the gospel or the name of Jesus is as responsible as anyone else. Not for failing to accept a message he has never heard, but for rejecting the knowledge of God revealed in creation. People do not suffer eternal exclusion from God for not having been born to the right parents in the right part of the world, but for rejecting that knowledge of God which is readily available to all.

God's Wrath Is Being Revealed from Heaven

The first thing we learn from Romans 1:18-20 is that God's wrath is being revealed from heaven. In verse 17 we read that God's righteousness is being revealed. These two statements should be understood in their relationship to each other. The question that arises is whether God's wrath as well as His righteousness is revealed in the gospel. Or, to put it another way, God's righteousness is revealed in the gospel but how is His wrath revealed? Some would say from the verses which follow that God reveals His wrath by giving men over to their depraved desires (see especially vv. 24, 26, and 28). God's anger is vented by His withdrawal from man. Mankind is abandoned by God to his own sinful desires. Since he insists on such things as sexual perversion and idolatry God lets him go his own way (note vv. 29-32).

A better interpretation, however (in that it maintains the parallelism between vv. 17 and 18), *is that the gospel itself reveals God's wrath*. In 2 Corinthians 2 Paul says that in preaching the gospel (see v. 12) he was the fragrance of Christ among those who were being saved and also among those who were perishing (see v. 15). To the latter the gospel was a "deadly fragrance that makes for death" and to the former "a vital fragrance that makes for life" (v. 16, *Moffatt*). The gospel reveals not only the love of God but also the consequences of rejecting such love. The "goodness" in good news is in direct proportion to the "badness" of refusing it. Shelter against a time of storm is meaningless in a land where it never rains. The gospel reveals not only the righteousness of God but also His wrath against those who refuse His offer of salvation.

Scholars often puzzle over the idea of a wrathful God. How can perfect love take revenge? Are not love and wrath mutually exclusive?

The answer lies in the realization that without righteous indignation against everything which would contravene His holiness, God could not be God in a moral universe. Consider the man who out of "love" for his wife would not protect her from attack. We would rightly describe such despicable action as cowardice of the most repugnant kind.

Genuine love requires righteous rejection of that which is essentially opposite to love. A holy God must hate sin in order to love righteousness. His character as God mandates it.

So we learn in the gospel that *God's wrath is revealed against all unrighteousness*. The good news carries the fragrance of death as well as the fragrance of life. What it means for each person is determined by one's personal response to the message. To a visitor in an art gallery who said he didn't like a certain classic painting came the response, "Sir, the pictures are not on trial, only the viewers." The gospel is not on trial. To accept it is to find revealed in it the righteousness of God. To reject it is to find revealed in it the wrath of God.

This wrath is said to be directed against "the godlessness and wickedness of men who suppress the truth by their wickedness" (Rom. 1:18). Note that man's attempt to stifle the truth of the gospel doesn't stem from a conviction based on logical argumentation. One would think that the truth or falsity of the gospel should be a matter for rational discourse. Ideally people discuss their differences and arrive at a mutually acceptable position. But that is not the way evil men carry out their campaign against the gospel. They try to suppress the truth *by wickedness*. In the following paragraphs we learn that man exchanged the "glory" of God for images (v. 23), the "truth of God" for a lie (v. 25) and "natural [sexual] relations" for lust, indecency and perversion (v. 27). This is his method for dealing with the question of truth. Unwilling to accept the truth he opposes it with every weapon of wickedness available.

Verse 19 is often held to show why God's wrath is now being revealed from heaven—that is, in spite of God's self-revelation man has turned his back on his Creator. It is better to interpret the verse as pointing out that man does have sufficient knowledge of the truth to justify the claim (in verse 18) that he is guilty of trying to suppress it. Unless God has revealed Himself, man obviously could not be guilty of suppressing any truth about Him. How could he?

God Has Revealed Himself to Mankind

Verses 19 and 20 are central to our discussion on the subject, "What Everyone Knows About God." The purpose of the section is not to set forth the basis for constructing a natural theology. We are not dealing with the question, Does God exist? We are asking, On what basis can it be said that people are morally responsible for suppressing the truth and consequently experiencing the wrath of God? Is God capricious in His righteous indignation? Is man the victim of not knowing what God requires?

The first thing we learn from verse 19 is that "what may be known about God is plain to them [men who would suppress the truth]." God is not unknowable. He has revealed Himself. Of course, this revelation is not a complete disclosure. Man in his finiteness could no more grasp all that God is than a child could understand the intricacies of the molecular theory or quantum mechanics. Such knowledge of God lies beyond human ken. Not until redeemed mankind stands face to face with eternal verities will partial knowledge give way to a more complete understanding of God and His ways. Paul writes, "Now I know in part; then I shall know fully, even as I am fully known" (1 Cor. 13:12). In a similar vein John adds, "We know that when he appears, we shall be like him, for we shall see him as he is" (1 John 3:2).

But simply because we cannot know everything about God does not imply that we can't know anything or that what knowledge we do have is necessarily distorted and unreliable. The doctrine of progressive revelation does not teach that as God gradually revealed more and more about Himself from the Garden of Eden to the cross of Calvary, a different sort of God finally emerged. The progressive nature of divine self-revelation means that the God who revealed Himself most completely in the incarnation of His Son is the same God who walked and talked with Adam and Eve in the garden. The progression has to do with the completeness of the revelation, not with any assumed change from one kind of a God to another.

So that which can be known of God by natural man (although minimal when compared to his self-revelation in Christ) has been made perfectly clear. It "lies plain before their eyes" (v. 19, *NEB*). Now, knowing means more than simply seeing. To know something about God is not merely to acknowledge observable evidence of His creative acts. Knowing involves interpretation and the inner compulsion to accept the implications of the evidence. Some translators have indicated this in their rendering of this passage. *Knox* says that what may be known about God "is clear to their minds." Even more specific is *Williams'* rendering—"is clear to their inner moral sense." They know in their hearts who God is and what He requires. The *NIV*'s "to them" is an interpretive translation of the Greek *en autois* (in them). Therefore, it is the image of God in man that equips him with the necessary moral and religious structure so that he clearly understands that which may be known about his Creator.

To guarantee the process God Himself took the initiative. All people have this basic knowledge of God because "God has made it plain to them" (v. 19). The emphasis is on God's involvement in the process. It was important to Him that there be a basis for moral judgment. Without revealing Himself He could hardly hold us responsible for not knowing who He is or what He requires. God does not judge a person for not responding to what he never had a chance to learn. In chapter 2 of Romans we read that those who sin under the law will be judged by the law, but those who sin apart from the law will perish apart from the law (see Rom. 2:12). The demands of God are that mankind respond according to the degree of knowledge and insight available to him in his own cultural and historic setting. This does not mean automatic salvation for the heathen; it only means that God's expectations conform to the degree of revelation that comes to each person. (Note in Romans 2:12 that those outside the law are *perishing*, not being saved.) We are not talking about salvation but about the basis for judgment.

We now come to the crux of the issue—verse 20. *Ever since the creation of the world certain of God's invisible attributes or perfections have been clearly seen.* Note the emphasis on the clarity—earlier writers called it perspicuity—of the divine revelation. Two are specifically mentioned: "his eternal power and divine nature." These perfections are said to be understood by means of what God has made.

Rational observation of the universe in which we live should provide all the proof necessary that creation does not provide the key to its own existence. What it does reveal is that the God behind it is a certain kind of God.

Mankind Is Without Excuse

Man is without excuse. By being made in the image of God he is equipped to interpret correctly the significance of the creation in which he finds himself. That which is speaks of a Creator whose power is eternal and whose nature is divine. This is the basis for our responsibility to accept the truth about God and conduct ourselves accordingly. Since mankind does not by nature do this, God is fully justified in exercising His wrath.

Several points in verse 20 deserve special attention.

First, knowledge of God has been available from the very first. The message is there. The creation itself is an expression of His nature and will. No one can say, I'm excusable because I lived in the dim, dark past before God actually began His work on behalf of man. In many ways, ancient man, with his immediate awareness of the physical world in which he lived, could see the revelation of God in nature more clearly than those who belong to a later period.

Second, God, being spirit (see John 4:24) cannot be seen and therefore is to be "observed" in what He has made and what He has done. "No one has ever seen God, but God the only Son . . . has made him known" (John 1:18). God is "the King eternal, immortal, *invisible*" (1 Tim. 1:17, italics added). Christ is "the image of the invisible God" (Col. 1:15). He is the visible imprint of the nature of God. As trees bent by the wind give evidence of an invisible force (the wind) so does nature bear the unmistakable signs of an invisible creator. But this Creator was not satisfied with such a minimal revelation of Himself, so in time He entered His own creation through the incarnation of His Son and explains to all who will listen exactly what He is like. Hebrews 1:1,2 says that after God spoke in the past at many times and in various ways, He has spoken to us in these last days "by his Son." That is, He has revealed Himself in the most complete and perfect way—by sending His Son who bears a flawless resemblance to the Father. If you know the Son you also know the Father (see John 14:7).

It is not on the basis of this fuller knowledge, however, that God holds mankind responsible. Man is without excuse because he rejects the basic knowledge of God which is available to everyone.

Thirdly, note that God's invisible qualities, which are clear on the basis of creation, are His eternal power and divine nature. I take this to mean that the evidence of creation propels a man persuasively toward the conclusion that the Creator is a powerful being and that this power is not in any sense limited in time. Earlier we talked about the inacceptability of the concept of the eternality of matter. The mind simply cannot conceive of matter as having existed forever, that is, *without beginning*. It is difficult enough to think of a supernatural being as having always existed. It is impossible to think of material stuff as having always been here. Creation demands a creator. This Creator who exists before what we call time is all-powerful. Creation teaches the unlimited might of the One who brought all things into being.

Further, the Creator is divine. He belongs to a higher sphere of existence. In Him we find the perfections which are reflected only dimly in the world around us. Our imperfect concepts of justice, love, and wisdom demand someone who is perfectly just, perfectly loving and perfectly wise. In the world which God has created we see evidence of a perfect God who gives us no other rational option but to confess His deity and observe the ethical implications which flow from that postulate.

So the end result is that men are without excuse. In their rebellion against the clear evidence of creation they are justly worthy of the wrath of God. This wrath has been revealed in the gospel. It is the "dark side" of God's love. Life is a serious matter. Our response to God's revelation determines whether the future for us is heaven or hell. The gospel is good news because it tells of God's provision for our need of absolute righteousness (which we find in Christ our substitute). It is "bad news" only in the sense that love refused results in wrath.

For Discussion

Most people find it difficult to think of a God of love who is also a God of wrath. The two qualities don't seem to go together. Love is tender and forgiving; wrath is aggressive and bitter. How can both of them coexist in God?

Is perhaps our understanding of love drawn from the way the concept is spelled out in secular thought? What about wrath? Does it differ from righteous indignation? Was Christ ever angry (see Mark 3:5)? What about Paul's instructions in Ephesians 4:26, " 'In your anger do not sin': Do not let the sun go down while you are still angry"? Does the fact that the Bible speaks of God anthropomorphically (as if He were man) have anything to do with how we should understand "wrath" when applied to God?

What kinds of things make you angry? Are these the things God wants you to be angry about?

2

When Man Turns His Back on God

Romans 1:21-32

In Romans 1:18-20 we learned that God's wrath against the unrighteousness of man is perfectly just. We cannot hide behind the claim that man doesn't know what God is like or what He expects of those created in His image. We are "without excuse" (Rom. 1:20). Creation itself reveals a Creator with "eternal power and [a] divine nature" (v. 20). Man has tried to "suppress" this knowledge (v. 18). His sin is not ignorance but willful rebellion.

What then shall we say about man in his natural state? When he "does what comes naturally" what does this reveal about his basic nature?

Romans 1:21-32 does not paint a pleasant picture. It describes in graphic detail the downward course of human conduct when God withdraws His presence and restraining influence. Not all men are as grossly sinful as the section portrays. Culture at times makes at least an outward difference. Social taboos sometimes prevent a people from degenerating as rapidly as they would in a non-restrictive situation.

The passage is, however, an accurate account of man's penchant for sin and willful rebellion. It tells us that when men turn from God they inevitably follow a downward course into degeneracy. If the verses strike you as extreme, remember that Paul is calling attention to an important theological doctrine (i.e., man's hopeless condition) without which there would be no real need for salvation. It is a vivid and dramatic way of saying that people by nature are lost—*really lost*!

All Men Have Knowledge of God

Running through the passage is the constant reminder that all men have knowledge of God. Verse 21 begins, "For although they knew God . . ." Verse 25 states that men "exchanged the truth of God for a lie." And again in verse 28 we learn that men "did not think it worthwhile to retain the knowledge of God."

It is important to keep this point clearly in mind. Man knows enough about God to be responsible. This means *all* men. In chapter 1 of Romans Paul is talking about the entire society in which he lived. These were not a favored few who had heard the gospel. They were simply people who lived and worked, fought and played in the first-century world. *They* are the ones with knowledge of God. By extension the group includes everyone everywhere at every point in time.

The subject of "Are the Heathen Lost?" often arises when believers get together to ponder the exclusive nature of the Christian faith. We question whether an aborigine who has never heard the name of Jesus will have to spend an eternity in hell for not accepting a Saviour he's never heard of. The answer is no. Heathen who end up apart from God will be there because they have failed to respond to the light which was given to them. In contrast to those who are under the law (and therefore will be judged by the law), "All who sin apart from the law will also perish apart from the law" (Rom. 2:12).

So bear in mind that *all men*, not merely those who have lived in the evangelized areas of the world, begin their journey with a knowledge of God.

Man Rebels Against God

To have knowledge in our possession does not necessarily mean we use it. Our basic problem is not ignorance but rebellion against truth. Wickedness would be far less blameworthy if we had no clear knowledge of right and wrong; to know God's requirements and flout them leaves no opportunity for us to plead indulgence.

From the very first, man has been a rebel. Placed in the Garden of Eden with everything supplied in abundance, Adam and Eve chose to believe Satan's lie that God was withholding something from them by restricting them from eating from the tree of the knowledge of good and evil (see Gen. 2:17). "Go ahead," said the serpent; "God has said no because He doesn't want you to have the advantage of being like Him" (see 3:1-5). So our first parents rebelled and the entire human race has suffered the effects of their rebellion (see Rom. 5:12).

Note specifically the nature of man's rebellion. Although he knows God he neither glorifies Him as God nor gives thanks to Him (see Rom. 1:21). To glorify is to bestow honor, to magnify, extol, or praise. Life in the age to come is described as a life of glory (see Luke 24:26). To glorify God is to ascribe to Him the perfections of His divine being as they are revealed now to the eye of faith but will be openly manifest in the eternal state.

It is appropriate for man to give thanks to God. In context, the giving of thanks stems from the realization of who God is as disclosed by what He has made. As man looks out into the vast reaches of space and marvels at the incredible power of the One who hurled the universe into place, it is reasonable that he should thank his Creator for the privilege of such a magnificent disclosure of divine power. In Carl Sagan's book *Cosmos* he states that a handful of sand contains about 10,000 more grains than the number of stars visible to the naked eye. Yet the total number of stars approximates the total number of grains of sand found on all the beaches of the entire planet earth. Imagine that!

And as man considers the intricacies of the human body, to say nothing of the subatomic world, it is reasonable that he should be grateful. The fact that the retina of the human eye contains some 7 million cones and 10 to 20 times that number of rods (for night and day vision) should cause a reasonable person to break out in thanksgiving for being a part of God's unimaginable creation.

But what does man do? He refuses to glorify God. He adamantly resists any temptation to express gratitude to his Creator. Face it—man is a rebel! Verse 23 tells us that "he exchanged [bartered off] the glory of the immortal God for images made to look like mortal man and birds and animals." He made a deal. He said, "Give me little graven images, it doesn't matter what they resemble—man, birds, animals, or even creeping things—and I'll give you the glory of God. I'm far more comfortable with what I can manipulate."

Verse 25 tells us about another trade-off: Man "exchanged the truth of God for a lie." Man knows the truth but he doesn't like it. Truth is uncomfortable because it bears witness against all untruth. It gives no quarter. Truth tells it like it is. To get ahead, man would rather tell it like it isn't. A little misrepresentation here, a little exaggeration there; here a partial truth, there an outright lie. Isn't that the way to make it to the top?

So man rebels against truth. It is simply too straightforward. He gladly swaps it for a lie. There now, isn't that better! Your evil disposition is your parents' fault. Your failure in business results from other people's unscrupulous actions. See how simple it is to impress the stranger by telling him of all the exploits which *could* have happened if only life had been more fair to you.

Man the rebel, how pitiful! Man, who began with a knowledge of God, "Did not think it worthwhile to retain the knowledge of God" (v. 28). Swallowing the deceitful lie of his worst enemy (Satan) he let go of the knowledge of God as a guide for life and conduct. Under the sway of satanic propaganda he decided on risking the ultimate shortcut. Duped by the enemy and driven by an intense desire to rule his own life man entered the ranks of the rebellious.

God's Response to Rebellion

What happens when man turns his back on God? While we know that God is infinite patience and desires all men "to come to repentance" (2 Pet. 3:9)—He is pictured in the parable of the prodigal son as a Father who eagerly and forgivingly awaits the return of the wayward (see Luke 15:20)—the present passage teaches that He is also a God who gives people up when they insist on pursuing their sinful ways. Three times in this passage in Romans we hear the solemn phrase, "God gave them up." In verse 24 God gave them over to sexual impurity. In verse 26 He gave them over to shameful lusts. In verse 28 He gave them over to a depraved mind.

Human freedom carries with it an awesome responsibility. To be free means to determine one's own destiny. God does not coerce man, nor bully him into accepting His love. God is a gentleman. He so loved mankind that He gave Himself in death that man might be freed from the penalty of sin (see John 3:16). But He never said, "Here, take this. You have no option but to believe."

But what if a person refuses to believe? Then a process of hardening sets in and man gradually develops a resistance to divine favor from which he cannot escape. He is hopelessly entrapped by his own decisions. From God's standpoint it is called God giving man up. From man's perspective it is the natural result of continuing to rebel against God. Yet it is more than the natural process of cause and effect. God actively decides to withdraw. As He gives man up, the process gradually takes over until it has run its full course.

In Hosea's charge against Israel the prophet says, "Ephraim is joined to idols; leave him alone!" (Hos. 4:17). Nothing can be done to change him. Freedom is dangerous business. Its alternatives bring blessing or disaster. While freedom provides man the opportunity to respond to God's offer of reconciliation, it also opens up the possibility that man will reject it.

Commentators have asked whether this divine withdrawal is complete or conditional. Has God totally and irrevocably given men up or has He, in the words of Isaiah, smitten them in order to heal? The prophet writes, "The Lord will strike Egypt with a plague; he will strike them and heal them. They will turn to the Lord, and he will respond to their pleas and heal them" (Isa. 19:22).

That plagues do not necessarily result in repentance is clear from the book of Revelation. Following the plagues of demonic locusts and fire-breathing cavalry in chapter 9, "The rest of mankind that were not killed by these plagues still did not repent" (Rev. 9:20). When pagan society determines willfully to pursue pleasure at any cost, it has, except in rare occasions, passed the point of no return. The decision to go on sinning in spite of the consequences seals a destiny. Such a person has committed the unpardonable sin (see Luke 12:10)—unpardonable not because God's forgiveness is unable to reach that far, but unpardonable because man is unable to ask for forgiveness. We will be what we are becoming!

Man Deceives Himself

I'm amazed at the number of words in the English language which carry the idea of deceit or deception. For the noun "deceit" one can substitute such terms as cunning, duplicity, guile, fraud, artifice, trickery, entrapment, and so on. The adjective "deceitful" has as synonyms such words as knavish, shifty, crafty, clandestine, and underhanded. "To deceive," the verb, may be said in many ways: to beguile, betray, four-flush, mislead, sell out, two-time, etc. "Deception" is chicanery, dishonesty, bamboozling, hoodwinking, and a score of similar terms.

Why does language have such a large supply of terms for such a questionable practice? Is it not that deceitfulness is such a central characteristic of our moral makeup? Not only does natural man make it a practice to deceive others, but in the very act he manages to deceive himself. Sin is a strange and sinister phenomenon. Although sinful acts are intended to hurt others they have a way of backfiring. Sin is a moral boomerang which inevitably harms the sinner more than the designated victim. Deception may fool the other for a time but it stains the deceiver in a permanent way. It is blood on the hands that will not wash—a disease which affects the carrier more than the victim.

Romans 1:21 says that although men knew God they neither glorified Him nor gave Him thanks and "hence all their thinking has ended in futility, and their misguided minds are plunged into darkness" (*NEB*). Goodspeed has them indulging "in futile speculation until their stupid minds have become dark." Man cannot reject truth and come away with clear and unaffected mental perception. To leave God, who is ultimate truth, is to lose touch with reality.

The terrifying thing about ignorance is that it is scarcely ever recognized by its victims. Verse 22 says that "although [men] claimed to be wise, they became fools." They are self-deceived; in their own judgment they have all the answers; they know what is best. But in fact they are fools. While a person's folly may in some cases consist in his inability to perceive the real issue (see Luke 11:40), more often it is the result of a wrong choice (see Luke 12:20). Willful rejection of the knowledge of God results in futile thinking and a darkened heart (see Rom. 1:21). The end of it all is a "depraved mind" (v. 28). Since they refuse the truth, God "allowed them to become the slaves of their degenerate minds" (*Phillips*).

What greater act of folly could there be than to exchange the truth for a warped and reprobate mind? Obviously those don't appear as the alternatives when a person makes his choice, but that does not alter the real situation. To turn from truth is to plunge oneself into darkness. Small wonder that most people's decisions are so regularly detrimental to their own welfare. Without direction there can be no progress. Without truth there can be only error.

God Condemns Two Notorious Vices

The passage we are dealing with doesn't make for pleasant reading. Sin has little to offer by way of an opportunity for cheerful discussion. Like Oscar Wilde's *Picture of Dorian Gray* the final revelation of sin is gross and repugnant. Paul does not hesitate to tell it like it is. His portrait of man in rebellion against God is anything but congenial.

The first major vice of verses 21-28 is "sexual impurity" (v. 24; the *NEB* has, "the vileness of their own desires"). *The Living Bible* translates the verse, "So God let them go ahead into every sort of sex sin, and do whatever they wanted to." Barclay speaks of this period of history as "An Age of Shame"—a time when men "degrad[ed] . . . their bodies with one another" (Rom. 1:24). Verses 26,27 are more explicit. God gives men over to "shameful lusts" (vile and disgraceful passions which bring dishonor). Paul adds, "Even their women exchanged natural relations for unnatural ones. In the same way the men also abandoned natural relations with women and were inflamed with lust for one another. Men committed indecent acts with other men, and received in themselves the due penalty for their perversion" (vv. 26,27).

Paul singles out homosexuality as the prime example of "disgraceful passions" (*Phillips*). Note what he says: (1) it is degrading (v. 24); it corrupts moral character and damages self-respect; it undermines self-esteem and brings dishonor. (2) It is contrary to nature (v. 26). It involves an essential perversion of the sex drive. Totally apart from any spiritual considerations, nature itself dictates that the appropriate sexual relationship is between male and female. (3) It results from an inflamed and indecent lust (v. 27). Montgomery speaks of those who are "ablaze with passion for one another" and Weymouth of those who "burned fiercely in their lust for one another." (4) It involves a penalty (v. 27). Paul is not speaking at this point of God's final judgment but of the natural penalty which accompanies the flouting of God's moral requirements. Sin carries its own penalty. In a moral universe the sinner pays in his own person the price of rebellion against his Creator.

From time to time some have accused Paul of exaggerating the moral degeneracy of the Greco-Roman world. Perhaps he was simply an overwrought moralist who got carried away by his own rhetoric. Not so. Barclay cites the secular writers of Paul's day who said the same things about society. Juvenal, the Roman satirist, tells of Agrippina, the wife of the emperor Claudius, who used to leave the royal palace at night and serve in a local brothel for the sake of sheer lust. Of the first 15 Roman emperors, 14 were said to be homosexuals. Nero was called every woman's man and every man's woman.

Homosexual practice was abhorred by the Jewish people. The men at Sodom and Gomorrah pressed Lot to deliver up his two angelic visitors "so that [they could] have sex with them" (Gen. 19:5). Lying with a man "as one lies with a woman" was detestable and ruled unlawful by Moses (Lev. 18:22). The New Testament holds the same attitude. When listing the wicked who will not inherit the kingdom of God, Paul cites "homosexual offenders" along with adulterers and the greedy (1 Cor. 6:9,10). In I Timothy 1:10 "perverts" are bracketed with adulterers and slave traders as that group for whom the law was made.

In recent years the subject of homosexuality has been widely discussed in America. The evangelical press has produced a number of books on the subject and opinion is somewhat divided. Is homosexuality genetically, psychologically, or culturally induced? Whatever the answer to that question there is no doubt that Scripture considers homosexuality a perversion of the natural order. To explain Romans 1:24-26 in such a way as to make sexual deviance acceptable to God when carried out in an atmosphere of love takes some rather nifty interpretive footwork.

The second major vice listed in this passage is idolatry. The "fools" of verses 22,23 exchanged the glory of the immortal God for "images made to look like mortal man and birds and animals and reptiles." After trading off the truth of God for a lie, man "worshiped and served created things rather than the Creator" (v. 25). Idolatry was the major sin of ancient Israel. Again and again she turned from God to worship idols. Pagan neighbors constantly undermined her fidelity to Yahweh by encouraging her to share in their worship of heathen gods.

The essential sin which gives rise to idolatry is selfishness. When a man creates his own god he can control it. It exists for his own pleasure and profit. This sort of god requires from him no particular standard of ethical or moral behavior. To worship an idol is ultimately to worship oneself. Idolatry is self-deification. Disguised as a religious exercise, idolatry finds wide approval as an acceptable form of worship. It debases because it obscures the revealed purpose of God and leads man to the blind conclusion that he can worship himself as a viable substitute.

Man at His Worst

Verses 29-31 are what is commonly known as a "catalog of vices"—a listing of the immoral habits and practices prevalent in pagan society. The vices listed in verses 24-28 were primarily sensual; the ones we now encounter are for the most part antisocial. (For similar lists see Gal. 5:19-21; 2 Tim. 3:2-5; etc.) Technical commentaries and theological wordbooks will describe each vice in detail. For our purpose it is enough to examine a few of the terms in order to gain a general impression of the society in which Paul lived. Recall that these characteristics come as the natural and inevitable result of man's rejection of the knowledge of God. This knowledge has been revealed to all men through creation. The image of God in man assures him that it is true.

Man is filled with "every kind of wickedness, evil, greed and depravity" (v. 29). Wickedness (*KJV*, "unrighteousness") is the opposite of equity, fair play. Evil is cruelty, the deliberate desire to harm another. Greed is that insatiable desire to have more. It tramples underfoot the rights of others in a frantic attempt to get ahead. Depravity (*KJV*, "maliciousness") is the complete absence of any redeeming virtue.

"They are full of envy, murder, strife, deceit and malice" (v. 29). Envy is resentful dislike of another because of advantage or possessions. It is a thoroughly nasty trait. Murder is wider than the act of manslaughter. It includes all the anger and hatred that lead a person to take the life of another. Strife is conflict that arises from base motivations and tears apart the structures of human relationships. Deceit is an expression of a warped mind plotting against the welfare of another. Malice translates a compound Greek word which means evil-natured. It describes the habit of putting the worst possible interpretation on the actions and words of others. It is human nature gone sour.

It is instructive that our catalog of vices contains a few signs which we within the believing community are apt to accept as relatively harmless—"gossips . . . insolent, arrogant and boastful." Surely these are excusable. Are they? Verse 32 states that God has righteously decreed that "those who do such things deserve death." How easy it is to gradually substitute our standards for God's!

God-haters are those who despise Him because He stands in the way of their full enjoyment of sin. Disobedience to parents is cited by Paul as one of the signs of the last days (see 2 Tim. 3:1,2). "Heartless" (Rom. 1:31) is better translated "without natural affection." Life in pagan society was cruel. We are told that infanticide was so common that every night 30 or 40 children were abandoned in the Roman forum. Weak or deformed babies were regularly drowned. "Ruthless" (without mercy or pity) describes the patrons who flocked to the gladiatorial games to watch men kill each other—a sport, it was called.

To do all these evil things is bad enough. To applaud the wickedness of others and in so doing help develop a public acceptance of vice and cruelty is even worse. It is an uncalled-for contribution to social degradation (see v. 32). To turn from God is to embrace darkness. The depth of man's fall can be measured only in terms of the potential he possesses for godliness. The habits of animals are not immoral—programmed by instinct they live as they do. For man, made in the image of God, to live like an animal is quite another story. In fact, the animal world is incapable of descending to the depths of man in revolt against God.

For Discussion

This has not been a pleasant discussion. It fills one with sadness to contemplate the moral depravity of man. Created to know and love God he ends up plagued with vice and suffering, the just recompense for his sin. He is *the Prodigal Son.*

Has Paul overstated his case? Are all people that bad? How many genuine derelicts do you know? Is sophisticated sin any less repulsive to God than flagrant and gross wickedness? Does God excuse sinners who live in nice houses and drive new cars while holding to account those who indulge in certain sins which society finds repugnant? In the long run does a gossip have a better chance of getting into heaven than a homosexual?

3

How God Makes Men Righteous

Romans 3:21-26

The theme of Romans is "good news." That is what the word *gospel* means. Originally gospel was *god spel,* that is, good tidings. Later it came to be used in the sense of God-story—the story of what God did to solve the problem caused by the sin and rebellion of mankind. Note that it is *good* news. It is a joyous proclamation that brings hope to all who recognize their lost condition. It tells of freedom for those in bondage, joy for those who sorrow and blessedness for the oppressed.

On the other hand, the gospel is not good news to those who don't want to hear it. A person determined to live a life of sin couldn't care less about the possibility of being freed from his vice. Those who don't know they are lost have no particular reason to be "saved." That is precisely why the first chapters of Romans focus on making all men aware of their need for righteousness.

The need for salvation does not depend upon a person's awareness of that need. Just before the Titanic was rammed by an iceberg and sent to its watery grave there was no particular awareness on the part of the passengers that they needed protection. That did not change the situation however. All men need God's forgiveness. Only those who recognize the need and act appropriately are in fact forgiven. To them the gospel is good news.

We read about this gospel in the very first verse of Paul's letter to the Romans. Paul is a servant of Christ Jesus set apart to announce "the gospel of God." It is then explained that the gospel was promised in the prophetic Scriptures of the Old Testament and centered on God's Son whose human lineage could be traced through David but whose divine nature was decisively declared by His resurrection from the dead (see Rom. 1:2-4).

This gospel is the theme of Romans and Paul is eager to make it known. He is "not ashamed of the gospel, because it is the power of God for the salvation of everyone who believes: first for the Jew, then for the Gentile" (Rom. 1:16). In this gospel is revealed "a righteousness from God" (v. 17). Scholars have long debated the exact meaning of this phrase. Cranfield is certainly correct in concluding that Paul is here speaking of a righteous standing for man made possible by God's redemptive action. This is what the gospel reveals—that God has provided a righteousness for man which has nothing to do with man's ethical achievements or religious and ceremonial activities. The righteousness of God is a right-standing which God bestows upon man. It is based on Christ's redemptive death and resurrection, and appropriated by faith and faith alone. It is a righteousness that is "by faith from first to last" (v. 17: "a process begun and continued by their faith," *Phillips*).

The New Righteousness

Now let us turn to the passage in Romans where the righteousness of God is described in detail (3:21-26). There is more theology compressed into these six verses than into any other comparable segment of Paul's writing. Here we encounter the central thrust of the apostolic message. In these verses he lays the foundation of his theology. To understand what Paul is teaching in this section is to have a firm grasp on the essence of the Christian faith. Everything else flows from this theological center.

Romans 3:19,20 sum up the long section, beginning with 1:18, on the hopelessness of man apart from God. The conclusion is that "no one will be declared righteous in [God's] sight by observing the law." To the contrary it is "through the law [that] we become conscious of sin" (v. 20).

Natural man has always tried to gain favor with his god by doing something which he believes will please him. The religions of the world are replete with examples of ritual acts thought to curry favor with the deity. Hindus have prayer wheels, Muslims bow down five times daily toward Mecca. Demon worshippers cut themselves in a frenzy of religious excitement, and Christians try to maintain regular attendance at church and be kind to their neighbors. In each case it is thought that if I only *do* the right things my god will accept me.

Righteousness—according to the vast majority of people who inhabit this globe—is something a person earns. It is a righteousness based on works. In Paul's day the Jews sought God's favor by religious and ceremonial activity. The Pharisees were a religious sect committed not only to the law as given by Moses, but to that vast body of oral tradition that had grown up over the years around the law. Paul concludes, however, that "whatever the law says, it says to those who are under the law, *so that* every mouth may be silenced and the whole world held accountable to God" (3:19, italics added). The purpose of the law is to make man aware of his need.

If man is unable to gain righteousness by strenuous moral effort, is there then any hope for him? Yes, of course, replies Paul. While it is certain that no one will be declared righteous as a result of obeying the law, there is a new righteousness available to man. Paul writes, "But now a righteousness from God, apart from law, has been made known" (3:21). A new stage has been reached. Law-righteousness has served only to make man more conscious of his sinfulness. The harder one tries, the more impossible it appears to be ever to stand before God fully accepted. The new righteousness, however, has nothing to do with human effort. It has its origin with God. It is something He confers.

It will be well to pause for a moment and distinguish between righteousness as an ethical concept and righteousness as right-standing before God. In the beatitudes when Jesus said, "Blessed are those who hunger and thirst for righteousness" (Matt. 5:6) He was speaking of the compelling desire to conduct one's life in an upright manner. This is ethical righteousness. On the other hand, when Paul in Romans 3 speaks of a "righteousness from God" he is using the term to mean the granting of a right-standing before God. The former has to do with conduct, the latter with status. God does not provide man with ethical righteousness. This is worked out in the life of the believer as a result of his being declared righteous in God's sight. Ethical righteousness (sanctification; discussed in Romans 6) develops as a result of positional righteousness.

The important thing about this new righteousness is that it is "apart from the law." That is, it is absolutely unearned. It does not result from keeping the law—doing the right thing. What a radical concept this would be to both Jew and Gentile—accepted by God on some basis other than human achievement! Yet this is exactly what the good news is all about. It is in fact the very reason *why* it is called *good* news. Since man as a result of his sinful nature will never be able to measure up to God's standards, God Himself will have to provide a way. Otherwise man will die in his sin. The gospel is the joyous declaration that God *has* done something—that He has provided acceptance on a basis that has nothing to do with our meager efforts.

Williams translates verse 21, "But now God's way of giving men right standing with Himself has come to light" (Montgomery strengthens the idea, "has been fully brought to light"). The gospel is a revelation. It unveils before our eyes what God has done on our behalf. It is a public declaration that what God requires He also provides.

While the gospel is good news, it isn't exactly new news. Paul goes on to say that "the Law and the Prophets testify" to this righteousness from God (v. 21). That the gospel is continuous with the Old Testament is pivotal in Paul's argument. In the very first sentence of his letter he establishes the point that the gospel was "promised beforehand through [God's] prophets in the Holy Scriptures" (Rom. 1:2). In chapter 4 the Old Testament patriarch Abraham is held up as the example of faith. Sections such as 10:16,17 and chapter 11 (where Israel, "the natural branches," will be grafted back into the olive tree into which the Gentiles, "wild by nature" had been grafted: vv. 17-24) tie together the Old and the New Testaments. The gospel—which reveals God's method of making men righteous—is no new departure. It is the clarification of a truth already known in earlier days. Exactly how God made clear the essential truth concerning His plan for man's deepest need will be seen when we consider verse 25.

Some attention should be given to the unfortunate

separation in the minds of many between the Old Testament and the New. The story of God at work in history to redeem for Himself a people who will renounce what they are by nature and allow God to make them into what He planned from the beginning runs throughout Scripture. It is the story of how God overcame man's sinful rebellion. It tells of God acting in history, first by calling out a people to be His own and in time by entering into His own creation to redeem mankind by the infinite sacrifice of Jesus Christ crucified, dead and buried. Without the New Testament the Old is a tragic story of frustrated expectations. Without the Old Testament the New is a strange conclusion to an unknown history. In God's plan the Testaments belong together. Together they form the complete account of God's good news. What we call the Old Testament is promise; what we call the New Testament is fulfillment.

The Role of Faith

So far we haven't answered the crucial question of how men receive this right-standing before God. Certainly it is not automatic; for this would mean that all men, whether they agreed to it or not, would be assigned to heaven. Yet at the same time it is not based on what a person is able to accomplish. If it is not based on works, what alternative is there?

The answer is found in verse 22: "This righteousness from God comes through faith in Jesus Christ to all who believe." Note three things.

First, a right-standing before God comes "through faith." Believing is the key. If you believe that God has accepted you, you are accepted. Faith is not a meritorious act—that is, it is not a good deed that merits some reward. Faith is simply an affirmative response to God's self-revelation. In chapter 4 of Romans we read that "Abraham believed God, and it was credited to him as righteousness" (4:3). In Genesis 15:5,6 we learn what he believed—specifically that his seed would be as the stars of the heaven (see Gen. 32:12 where the metaphor is changed to "sand of the sea"). Abraham's response to God was affirmative and God proclaimed him righteous.

This brings us to our second point. *Following the incarnation, death and resurrection of Christ Jesus, the gospel has come into sharp focus.* Now God declares righteous those who have "faith in Jesus Christ." He is the object of our faith, the final and supreme revelation of the nature of God, "the exact representation of his being" (Heb. 1:3). Ever since the cross, God asks us to believe in His Son. Righteousness comes through faith in Jesus Christ. This means that we must respond with full confidence to who Jesus is and what He did for the salvation of mankind. He is named Jesus "because he will save his people from their sins" (Matt. 1:21) and He is designated Christ, the anointed one, who has faithfully carried out the redemptive mission assigned to Him.

And thirdly, this right-standing before God is available "to all who believe." God's plan is inclusive. From God's standpoint no one is excluded. Among the great throng which will ultimately stand before Him in eternity will be those from "every nation, tribe, people and language" (Rev. 7:9). God has no barriers—ethnic, political, economic, or social. The sole distinguishing characteristic of the righteous is that they believe in Jesus Christ. Later on Paul will stress what faith involves by way of conduct. For the moment he needs to state as clearly and unambiguously as possible the crucial nature of faith. The sole prerequisite for acceptance before God is to believe His promise. "Faith alone" was the theological cornerstone of the Reformation. Over against the gradual eclipse of this fundamental Pauline doctrine, Luther and others opened a new day by reasserting that man is saved by faith alone. Needless to say, they found their mandate in Romans and Galatians.

Paul once again emphasizes that all men need the righteousness of God. No one is accepted on his own merits. Both Jew and Gentile stand guilty before God. "There is no difference, for all have sinned and fall short of the glory of God" (Rom. 3:22,23). There are two ways to interpret this statement. It may be viewed in reference to the life of the individual. Every person in the world has at sometime sinned and therefore falls "short of God's glorious ideal" *(TCNT)*. God intended us to be like Him. The first moment in which we sinned we became unlike Him and fell short of His divine intention. This approach is supported by the fact that while the first verb is aorist *(past tense)* the second is present. We *continue* to fall short of His glorious ideal.

Although this makes sense and is certainly an accurate picture of man, a second interpretation is probably what Paul intended. Elsewhere Paul teaches that "it is certain that death reigned over everyone as the consequence of [Adam's] fall" (Rom. 5:17, *JB*). The doctrine of corporate headship implies our involvement in Adam's sin. (Note that it is on the same basis that we can claim to be righteous. Christ is our new corporate head! (See Rom. 5:19.) In this sense we sinned in Adam. As a consequence we "are deprived of the divine splendour" (3:23, *NEB*). The "glory of God" is the divine radiance with which Adam was created and which he lost through his rebellious decision against God. It is this same glory which is to be restored in the coming age. Paul calls it a splendor not worthy of comparison with "our present sufferings"

(8:18). It is a glory to be revealed in that great eschatological moment when creation itself will be liberated from the bondage of decay and brought into the "glorious freedom of the children of God" (8:21).

Some writers take Romans 3:22b,23 as a parenthesis and make verse 24 carry on the thought of verse 22a ("to all who believe . . . and are justified freely"). This arrangement eases the problem caused by the apparent implication that the "all" who have sinned (v. 23) are also "justified freely by his grace" (v. 24: universal salvation?). It is better to link verse 24 directly with verse 23 but to understand that while all have fallen short of the glory of God only those who believe are freely justified. That faith is the sole means of justification is central to the entire section and should be assumed in verse 24.

Word Pictures by Paul

At this point Paul gives us some of his most profound insights into the redemptive work of God. To do so he uses several metaphors. He borrows images from the practice of law (acquittal of the guilty), the custom of buying slaves (redemption), and the ritual practices of sacrifice (atonement). All of these figures are brought together in verses 24,25. No wonder Paul has been dubbed "the master of mixed metaphors"!

In the first place, Paul writes, the sinner who places his trust in Jesus Christ is "justified freely by his grace." To be justified means to be acquitted, to gain a right standing. Justification frees the guilty man from paying the just penalty for his sin. It declares that he is totally exonerated. All charges are dropped. This acquittal is absolutely free because it is based on the unmerited favor (grace) of God. God decided to set man free, arranged a plan by which He could justify the guilty and still remain a moral being, and then carried it out. It's a free offer. The only option we have is to accept or reject it.

You would think that sinners would love to be forgiven at no cost. Not so. After all, natural man has his sinful pride. He desperately wants to claim some role in his own redemption. He resists being placed in the position of needing to declare absolute moral bankruptcy. How face-saving it would be if man could work out a cooperative arrangement with God. Salvation by joint effort would give the sinner some credit for personal achievement. Unacceptable, says God. To be lost means to be lost! There is no way to struggle up out of quicksand. Either you allow me to do it *all* or no help is available. Why is God so firm on this point? Because in heaven all glory and honor and praise belong to God. There will be no swapping of stories there about how we helped God.

Secondly, justification is ours "through the redemption that came by Christ Jesus" (v. 24). While some have argued that "redemption" means no more than deliverance, it is worth noting that the Greek word (a compound noun) has as its base the specific idea of a ransom paid for the freeing of a slave or for captives taken in war. To redeem means to buy back. "You are not your own," says Paul; "you were bought at a price" (1 Cor. 6:19,20). To be redeemed means to have been freed from the marketplace of sin by the payment of a ransom. The price was paid by the One who came not to be served but "to give his life as a ransom for many" (Mark 10:45). Questions regarding to whom the ransom was paid push the metaphor beyond what it was intended to teach.

The third image is drawn from ceremonial practice. *"God presented him [Christ Jesus] as a sacrifice of atonement"* (Rom. 3:25). *This last phrase has received an enormous amount of scholarly attention. The KJV trans-*

lates "sacrifice" as "propitiation"; the *RSV* "expiation." The former suggests that there was something in the death of Christ which propitiated or appeased the righteous anger of God. The latter carries the idea of covering sins. The word in the Greek Old Testament translates a Hebrew term for the lid of the Ark (the mercy seat). Herrmann, in Kittel's famous *Theological Dictionary of the New Testament* (vol. 3, p. 319), notes that the term means an "atoning headpiece" and according to certain passages appears not to be a part of the Ark itself (see for example Exod. 30:6). In either case, however, the important point is that it is the place where atonement is made.

In Jewish practice the high priest entered the Holy of Holies once a year and sprinkled blood above the Ark for the atonement of Israel's sins. What Paul is saying is that Jesus is that "mercy seat"—that meeting place between God and man where the great and final eternal sacrifice has been made. The death of Christ expiates or covers the sins of man and at the same time propitiates the righteous anger of God (against sin and its consequences, not against the sinner per se).

This great redemptive work of Christ is appropriated by man "through faith in his blood" (v. 25). What we today are called upon to believe is the effectiveness or sufficiency of that death. That Christ died is a historically verifiable fact; that His death provides forgiveness for sin is an interpretation that we accept by faith. Apart from trust in the significance of Christ's death (and resurrection) there is no forgiveness for sin—no way of gaining a right standing before God.

The Divine Dilemma
Paul now adds that God set forth His Son as a propitiatory sacrifice in order "to demonstrate his justice" (v. 25;

repeated in v. 26). How did the death of Christ display the justice of God? Since "in His forebearance God had passed over the former sins of men in the times that are gone by" (v. 25, *Conybeare*) it could be questioned whether God had in fact acted justly. Would not such a passing over of sin be incompatible with God's perfect justice? Not at all, in that the sacrifice of Christ itself is clear evidence that God views sin with ultimate seriousness. He may have "passed over" the sins of former times but he didn't "forgive and forget." If He had not taken sin seriously He would not be a moral God. If Christ had not died for sin there could have been no forgiveness. For this reason it was necessary for God to provide a lasting basis for forgiveness and reconciliation.

In addition to providing the basis for man's redemption the death of Christ also vindicated the justice of God. "He did it to demonstrate his justice at the present time, so as to be just and the one who justifies the man who has faith in Jesus" (v. 26). This then is God's ultimate purpose in openly setting forth His Son as an offering of atonement.

As we mentioned at the outset, Paul in this one paragraph has provided a crystal clear and remarkably comprehensive summary of the gospel. Here is the ultimate good news. Although its theology is compressed, the message is clear. Let's lay it out in outline form.

The righteousness of God is

1. from God
2. apart from law
3. testified to in the Old Testament
4. through faith in Jesus Christ
5. needed because all have sinned
6. based upon grace
7. achieved through the sacrificial death of Christ

8. not jeopardized by God's having passed over former sins.

The gospel declares that God is righteous and has provided through the death of His Son a right standing for all who will believe. This message thrust the early church out into the mainstream of the first centuries of the Christian era and established against all odds a firm foundation for the historical growth of the church. The gospel is great and glorious good news!

For Discussion

Romans 3:21-26 is New Testament theology (soteriology, that is) at its best. It deals with profound ideas. It explains the purpose of God in eternity and provides a rationale for the most awesome event in time. Although sinful men crucified the Son of God, that very event has become the basis for their forgiveness.

Does all this have any relevance for what we call "real life"? Does it make any difference in how we meet the trials and traumas of existence in the twentieth century? Perhaps we need more "practical" help? Wouldn't a talk on overcoming stress or bringing up teenagers be more helpful? Is there any place for theology in today's church, especially since it is so difficult to cope with the problems created by a disturbed and misguided society?

Or is it possible that theology is somehow related to ethics at a strategically important level? Could ethics exist apart from a theological foundation? Without a standard (a theology) can anyone seriously say what people *ought* to do? Could there be Christian morals without Christian theology? Does Peter's statement, "Be holy, because I am holy" (1 Pet. 1:16) have any bearing on the answer? Would you agree that every imperative must rest on an indicative?

4

Abraham: Man of Faith

Romans 4:1-25

Up to this point Paul has been writing about justification by faith in fairly abstract and theological terms. Most people can grasp an idea more easily when it is seen in the context of real life. Embodied in a person, truth becomes clear and persuasive. So Paul moves the discussion from the conceptual to the concrete. In 3:28 he had drawn the conclusion that "a man is justified by faith apart from observing the law." God is therefore God of both Jew and Gentile. To illustrate this central truth he turns to the experience of Abraham, that great Old Testament exemplar of faith and obedience.

Chapter 4 divides into three basic parts. Verses 1-8 establish the point that Abraham was justified, not by works, but by faith. Verses 9-17 underscore the fact that Abraham is the father of all who believe, both Jew and Gentile. Since God declared him righteous *before* he was circumcised he is the father of *all* the faithful. Furthermore, the promise did not rest on Abraham's observance of the law but on the grace of God. Verses 18-25 provide important insights into the nature of Abraham's complete confidence in God and point up its relevance for us today.

How Abraham Was Made Righteous Before God

Abraham was the first patriarch of Hebrew tradition, the father of the Jewish race. His life of faithful obedience was "rooted in fellowship with the unseen" (John Bright). He was, as James puts it, "God's friend" (Jas. 2:23). Through the centuries he has been appropriately considered the finest example of absolute confidence in God.

When Paul referred to Abraham in support of his view that man was made righteous by faith rather than works, the apostle's Jewish contemporaries saw him playing into their hands. He even quoted one of their crucial passages in support of his thesis: Genesis 15:6, "Abraham believed God, and it was credited to him as righteousness" (Rom. 4:3; see also Jas. 2:23). But had God not promised that Abraham's descendants would be as numerous as the stars and that through his offspring all nations would be blessed "*because Abraham obeyed* me and kept my requirements" (Gen. 26:4,5, italics added)? Was it not, therefore, *because of Abraham's obedience* that he was declared righteous? Doesn't this prove that Abraham was declared righteous on the basis of something he did? (The fact that Abraham lived hundreds of years before the giving of the law and therefore could not keep it in any literal way was solved by the rabbis who taught that he kept it by anticipation.)

By quoting Genesis 15:6 Paul takes a basic proof text of Judaism and shows that when properly interpreted it supports the exact opposite of what the Jews understood. Note that the passage itself says nothing more than that Abraham "believed God" and it was credited to him as righteousness. If something else beyond believing were required it would have been mentioned. God had taken Abraham outside the tent and shown him the innumerable stars of heaven. Count them if you can, God challenged.

"So shall your offspring be" (Gen. 15:5). Then follows verse 6. Abraham believed God "and his faith was regarded by God as righteousness" (Rom. 4:3, *TCNT*). Scripture is perfectly clear: God declares that those who place their full confidence and trust in Him are accepted in His sight. It is not by doing, but by believing, that men are made righteous.

That God accepts sinners on the basis of faith alone is undoubtedly the most unacceptable truth ever laid before religious man. Pride demands that we earn acceptance. Pride refuses to admit that it is morally bankrupt, that no matter how hard it tries it can never merit at least some measure of divine favor. It is absolutely unaware of the great gulf that stands between man's best efforts and God's nonnegotiable requirements.

The sign on the beach said, "Lifeguard wanted: must be six feet in height." Small boys playing in the sand may decide that Johnny will surely get the job because he is an inch taller than the others. Unfortunately he is still only four feet tall! Pride measures its accomplishments against the "merits" of others. God requires perfection, and that perfection exists only in Christ. By faith in *Him* we receive *His* merit. We are "accepted in the beloved" (Eph. 1:6, *KJV*). Like Abraham we are declared righteous by believing God; nothing more, nothing less.

Verses 4-8 go on to point out that whatever a man receives for what he does cannot be considered as a gift. It is something he earned. An obligation is involved. If God were to accept us on the basis of our work then salvation could not be considered a gift; it would be something that God would owe us. This would leave pride intact. Man could flaunt his independence in the face of his Creator.

Paul supports his position by referring to Psalm 32. David had made the same point when he spoke of "the blessedness of the man to whom God credits righteousness apart from works" (Rom. 4:6). Commentators call attention to Paul's use of a rabbinical principle of interpretation by which two passages are allowed to illuminate each other whenever the same word occurs in each. As applied at this point the conclusion is that "counting righteous" (see v. 3) is the equivalent of "not counting sin" (see v. 8). Thus, blessed is the man who is forgiven/ whose sins have been covered/whose sins the Lord will never count against him, because this is the man who believes God and it is counted to him as righteousness.

Why Abraham Is the Father of All Who Believe

In the same way that Romans 4:1-8 expand Romans 3:28, verses 9-17 of chapter 4 enlarge upon Romans 3:29 ("Is God the God of Jews only? Is he not the God of Gentiles too? Yes, of Gentiles too."). As before, the faith of Abraham provides the basis for discussion.

The first point Paul establishes in his argument that Abraham is the father of all who believe is that the patriarch was still uncircumcised at the time when God declared him to be righteous. The chronology is strategic. Abraham is declared righteous in chapter 15 of Genesis. In the *following* chapter he is said to be 86 when his son Ishmael was born (see Gen. 16:16). Abraham is instructed to undergo circumcision in Genesis 17:11, which act is performed (according to Gen. 17:24-26) when he is 99 and his son is 13. Whether or not the rabbis were correct in counting exactly 29 years between Genesis 15:6 and 17:11 is not especially important. The important point is that Abraham's circumcision *followed* by a number of years his being declared righteous by God. In respect to his religion he was still a Gentile when God accepted his act of faith and pronounced him righteous.

This is an unanswerable argument. It was a decisive blow against all who believed that God's blessings came automatically to the Jew and that circumcision was the essential proof that one belonged to the favored few. So important had the rite of circumcision become that according to some rabbis should it ever be necessary for God to condemn a Jew he would send an angel ahead of time to make the culprit uncircumcised before consigning him to punishment.

Paul's line of argument jolted his Jewish protagonists into the realization that the very first Jew, the venerable Abraham, father of the Jewish race, was indeed a Gentile when God pronounced him righteous. All their cherished notions about earning God's favor would have to be discarded. It is by faith that God accepts man. And since it is by faith alone it follows that God must be the God of all who believe. Although the Jews had been greatly privileged down through history, they still could come to God only by believing. All their works of righteousness were so much ritual baggage. They had no corner on God. He was Creator of all men everywhere and Father of all who placed their trust in Him. Circumcision was no more than "the stamp of God's acknowledgment of the uprightness based on faith that was his [Abraham's] before he was circumcised" (Rom 4:11, *Goodspeed*).

The logical conclusion begins in the middle of verse 11: "So then, he is the father of all who believe but have not been circumcised . . . and he is also the father of [those] who not only are circumcised but who also walk in the footsteps of the faith that our father Abraham had before he was circumcised" (4:11,12). To "walk in the footsteps" of Abraham means to join the ranks of the faithful. Jews allowed Gentiles to enter their company if they would undergo circumcision, be baptized, and accept the ceremonial obligations of Judaism. Paul now tells the Jews that in order to join the company of Abraham they will have to come by the way of faith alone, apart from any obligation of the law. They will have to walk in Abraham's footsteps.

Paul's second point, in support of the thesis that God is the father of all who believe, is that God's "promise was made on the ground of faith [not on the observance of law], in order that it might be a matter of sheer grace" (4:16, *NEB*). The argument runs from verse 13 through the first half of verse 17.

The promise to Abraham and his descendants that he would inherit the world did not come as a result of their keeping the law (see 4:13). The promise Paul refers to is probably Genesis 22:17,18, "I will surely bless you and make your descendants as numerous as the stars in the sky and as the sand on the seashore . . . and through your offspring all nations on earth will be blessed." Certainly, then it would be argued, the promise rests upon works because it is followed with the clear statement that Abraham's blessing was a result of his obedience: Genesis 22:18 closes with the words, "because you have obeyed me." Earlier in the same chapter we read of Abraham's crucial test of faith. God tells him to take his only son Isaac to Mount Moriah and sacrifice him there as a burnt offering. Abraham obeys and at the last moment God stays his hand and provides a ram for sacrifice (see Gen. 22:1-14). According to Jewish thought this act of Abraham was considered to be of supreme merit.

But promise does not rest upon obedience. It came through the uprightness that Abraham had as a result of his faith (Rom. 4:13). If only a select group of lawkeepers are heirs to the promise, then "faith has no value and the promise is worthless" (4:14). You cannot have it both

ways. If righteousness comes by faith alone then it
doesn't belong to those who rely on keeping the law.
Observance of law as a way to gain God's favor empties
its meaning. In that case a promise which rested upon
faith would be worthless (v. 14). Law and promise are
essentially antagonistic. Law deals in meritorious activity; promise rests on the free grace of God.

It is worth pointing out that in the Greek language
there are two words for promise. One has to do with a set
of conditions and amounts to little more than the keeping
of a contract ("If you do thus and so then I will promise to
do something."). The other (and this is the term used here)
refers to a spontaneous promise made out of the goodness
of one's heart. It is not qualified by a set of conditions.
God's promise to Abraham was not a legalistic negotia-
tion involving terms on God's part. It was the free and
uncaused expression of His intention to bless Abraham
and through his descendants to bless all mankind. All the
best promises are like that!

Law was never intended to result in promise. To the
contrary, "Law brings wrath" (v. 15). Instead of providing man the means to lay claim on God's blessing, law
turned sin into conscious transgression and provoked an
even more serious situation.

Because the promise rests on faith it "may be guaran-
teed to all Abraham's offspring" (v. 16). God's justifying
man is an act of sheer grace. There is nothing in man that
calls forth this saving act. Man's sole responsibility is to
reach out in faith—to believe that God is both willing and
able to do what He has promised. Right-standing before
God is not a reward for having met some standard of
ethical behavior. Right-standing before God is a gift.
"Nothing in my hands I bring; simply to thy cross I cling,"
is how the songwriter puts it. Since faith is the sole

requirement, no one may be excluded on the basis of a set of ceremonial prescriptions. Citing Genesis 17:5 Paul concludes, "As it is written: 'I have made you a father of many nations' " (Rom. 4:17). Abraham is the father of all who believe.

What Abraham's Faith Was Like

In the last verse of the preceding section God was described as "the God who gives life to the dead and calls things that are not as though they were" (4:17). Abraham's faith rested in a miracle-working God. Strong confidence in who God is, and therefore in what He is able to do, determined the way Abraham met the challenge to believe "against all hope" (v. 18).

Note the paradox in verse 18: "With no ground for hope, Abraham, sustained by hope, put faith in God" (*TCNT*). Based on human calculation there was no hope. Abraham fell on the floor laughing when God promised that Sarah would bear a child (see Gen. 17:17). The idea was preposterous for Sarah as well. Abraham was 100 and she was 90. Sarah asked rather skeptically, "After I am worn out and my master is old, will I now have this pleasure?" (Gen. 18:12). Yet Scripture reports that Abraham "in hope believed" (Rom. 4:18). As long as he looked at the "impossibility" from a human standpoint it remained just that. But sustained by a hope that rested firmly in God he believed that the "impossible" was possible. In fact he was thoroughly convinced that it would surely come to pass.

Although Abraham's "body was as good as dead . . . and . . . Sarah's womb was also dead . . . he did not waver through unbelief regarding the promise of God" (vv. 19,20). With all the odds against him Abraham refused to lose confidence in God's promise. He was "fully persuaded" (v. 21). This tenacious confidence in the character and word of God was counted "to him as righteousness" (v. 22).

In Abraham we have a marvelous example of what it means to believe in God. God does not ask us to affirm the impossible just because it is impossible. He does require, however, that our confidence in what He has promised is greater than any obstacle which life is able to place in our path. For Abraham the obstacle was the simple fact that both he and Sarah were past the age of bearing children. Nature said no, but God said yes. Whom should he believe? God, of course.

Abraham's faith was not irrational. It was not a blind leap into the dark. His faith was supremely rational. Is it unreasonable to believe that the Creator of all there is is able to do something out of the ordinary? Is God a prisoner of the way He normally acts? Have the "laws of nature" (man's generalizations about how God normally acts in nature) backed the Creator into the corner? Have they tied His hands? No. When God enters the equation anything is possible. Abraham believed God and this confidence was "credited to him as righteousness" (v. 22).

The last three verses of chapter 4 stress that what we have learned about Abraham is intended for us as well. God's ways with man follow a predictable pattern. From the very first God wanted man of his own free will to trust Him. In the Garden, Satan sowed doubt in the mind of Eve—"Did God really say . . . ?" (Gen. 3:1). The suggestion created for Eve a genuine crisis of belief. God had said, "Trust me." Satan said, "God can't be trusted." The first rebellion in the history of man was instigated by the subtle lie of Satan. Century after century of sorrow has followed in the wake of man's first decision not to trust God.

Now God comes to man, having given His Son as a sacrifice for man's rebellion, and says, "Trust me. You can never earn my forgiveness but you can receive it as a free gift if you will only believe. Abraham trusted my word when I said he would have innumerable descendants. Will you trust me now when I tell you that Christ Jesus was delivered over to death for your sins and was raised to life for your justification? As Abraham believed and was counted righteous, so also will you stand before me in righteousness if you simply believe."

You will have noted that what we are asked to believe differs from what Abraham believed. For him it was the promise of a son; for us it is the fact that Christ died for sin and was raised again. In both cases, however, the important thing is to have confidence in what God has said. To "walk in the footsteps of the faith [of] Abraham" (Rom. 4:12) means to believe *as* he believed (not *what* he believed).

For Discussion

The subject of faith alone as God's method of crediting man with righteousness has been dealt with as extensively as possible. It is the controlling idea of the first four chapters of Romans. After being stated as clearly as possible in theological terms (see 3:21-26) it is illustrated by an extended discussion of Abraham, the man of faith.

Why is it, do you think, that people still have a hard time understanding how a person is made right before God? Why is it so difficult to accept the fact that God requires absolutely nothing from us for salvation other than faith? Reflect on what you know about other religions and fill in the blanks:

According to _____ [name of religion] man is saved by _____. Is the answer works or faith? Do you know any other religion that holds out the good news that salvation is not by striving but by accepting what God has done on our behalf?

How Christian is the statement, "Ask not what you must do for God; ask rather what God has done for you"? If you went out today and asked 10 people on the street how to gain God's favor, how many, do you suppose, would answer something like, "By *doing* a lot of good things"? On the basis of Romans 4 how would you answer them?

5

The Benefits of Believing

Romans 5:1-11

For a logical and orderly presentation of the Christian faith there is no better book than Paul's letter to the church in Rome. It is the best piece of literature available for the unbeliever desiring a succinct and authoritative statement of what it means to be a Christian. Remember that Paul wrote *letters*, not theological monographs intended for publication. Yet we cannot help but marvel at the depth of theological insight and the far-reaching consequences of what at its time of writing must be taken as incidental literature. While God is the ultimate author of all New Testament Scripture, it is still amazing that so much of that which is absolutely central to the Christian faith could be set forth so clearly in such a relatively short document.

Chapters 5-8 form the second major division of the book of Romans. After some introductory remarks and a statement of the book's theme—1:1-17—Paul establishes the need of all men for righteousness and explains how this righteousness has been supplied in Christ Jesus—1:18-3:31. Chapter 4 illustrates the crucial point he made in 3:22—that the righteousness which is from God comes to man "through faith in Jesus Christ"—by turning to Abraham, the Old Testament exemplar of faith.

The theme of chapters 1-4 was justification by faith. Chapters 5-8 represent a second stage in Paul's presentation. Now we learn how those who have been declared righteous by God are to live. What are the ethical implications that necessarily follow from the truth just established, i.e., that by faith sinners are made righteous in the sight of God? This section (chapters 5-8) presents the logical connection between justification and sanctification. It provides a philosophical-religious perspective for living out our justification. Later in the book (chapters 12-15) Paul will deal more specifically with ethical injunctions. Here he is intent on clarifying the necessary relationship between believing and living. He begins the section by bringing out the benefits of believing. The benefits discussed in verses 1-11 are seven in number.

We Have Peace with God

"Therefore, since we have been justified through faith, we have peace with God through our Lord Jesus Christ" (5:1).

Peace is one of those pleasant words which conjure up images such as summer twilight on the shore of a placid lake. It speaks of tranquility in the midst of turmoil and strife. It promises repose, the stilling of anxiety. Obviously, the word is sufficiently broad to be used in all such settings.

The biblical idea of peace, however, is a much less subjective concept. *Shalom*, the Hebrew word for peace (used as a common greeting in modern Israel) has as its basic meaning the idea of well-being. God, through Isaiah, tells Israel, "If only you had paid attention to my commands, your peace would have been like a river" (Isa. 48:18)—you would have prospered and all would have been well with you. In the New Testament *eirēnē* (peace) normally carries all the connotations of its Old Testament counterpart. To be at peace with God means that hostility has ceased and access into His presence has been established.

This is what Paul has in mind in Romans 5:1 when he writes that those who are justified through faith "have peace with God." Man the sinner has fallen under the wrath of God. By his rebellion he has made himself an enemy of God. But God, by the sacrifice of His Son, paid the price of man's redemption. No longer an enemy, man may now find himself at peace with God. Obviously, such a state of well-being is not automatic. It comes as a result of believing. It is faith's first great benefit.

The author of Hebrews reminds us that Christ became "a high priest forever, in the order of Melchizedek" and that Melchizedek's title, king of Salem, means "king of peace" (Heb. 6:20; 7:2). God Himself is the "Lord of peace" who gives "peace at all times and in every way" (2 Thess. 3:16). Against this background the peacemakers whom Jesus declares blessed in Matthew 5:9 are not those who help others settle little squabbles (as good as that may be) but those whose energies are used to bring men to salvation—to that state of well-being which God calls peace.

A word about the translation of Romans 5:1. Although the better manuscripts have "we have peace," others have "let us have peace" (note the margin or footnote in the *NIV*). The difference hinges upon whether the verb is spelled with an omicron (short o) or an omega (long o). Since they sound very much the same and scribes often "copied" by ear from a reader, the mistake could easily occur. Some modern translators, not wanting to give up either idea, have come up with a collated version. (*Phillips*, for example, has, "Let us grasp the fact that we have peace." *Montgomery* has, "Let us continue to enjoy the peace we have.")

We Have Access into His Grace

"We have peace with God through our Lord Jesus Christ, through whom we have gained access by faith into this grace in which we now stand" (Rom. 5:1,2).

It is through Christ that believers have gained access to God. The word "access" is interesting. The verb form is used of being ushered into the presence of royalty. To "gain access" describes the entrance of a person into the immediate presence of someone of high standing. We speak of people having an "audience" with the king. The word may be used appropriately to describe man's approach to God. Ephesians 3:12 says that through faith in Christ "we may approach God with freedom and confidence."

Remember that by basic temperament we are "natural enemies" of God. We do not seek His favor (read again Romans 3:10-18). It was our hostility that separated us from Him. Yet He paid the price of our rebellion. He satisfied His own righteous nature by becoming sin for us (see 2 Cor. 5:21) and now freely offers us access. The door is open; the King is on His throne. The heralds have sounded their trumpets and we stand about to enter. By faith we have access. It is our privilege—rebels that we are—to step into God's presence by faith and enjoy forever the inheritance of eternal joy.

Paul refers to this as the "grace in which we now stand" (Rom. 5:2). This grace is more than the objective fact that we are forgiven. It involves the full enjoyment of our new position. God has graciously invited us to be His special friends. We may therefore enter at will into His royal throne room. He wants us to enjoy the freedom to come and go as we desire. We have *taken our stand* (the Greek verb is in the perfect tense indicating an action of the past whose influence continues in the present) by faith. As children of the King we are free to approach without fear or reticence. Hebrews puts it aptly, "Let us then approach the throne of grace with confidence, so that we may receive mercy and find grace to help us in our time of need" (Heb. 4:16).

Some writers see a slightly different image in Romans 5:2. In later Greek the word for "access" was used of a harbor, the place where a ship could enter and escape the storms of the open sea. Man intent on establishing his own righteousness is like a ship tossed about by the angry waves. The harder he tries, the more he is at the mercy of the storm. It is by entering the harbor of God's grace that he finds salvation. Faith is simply the decision to head for that haven. It discovers that the harbor does the saving. It is an "access" which brings an end to striving. It is man's natural tendency to struggle for himself that keeps him from the quiet waters of God's provision. How much simpler to enter by faith than to flounder in the open sea of self-dependence.

We Rejoice in Hope

"And we rejoice in the hope of the glory of God" (Rom. 5:2). "Character [produces] hope. And hope does not disappoint us" (5:4,5).

When Paul wrote about rejoicing "in the hope of the divine splendour" (*NEB*) which awaited the righteous (those who by faith had acquired a right standing before God), his words would have made a special impact on Christians at Rome who lived in the midst of a Greco-Roman culture that viewed hope in quite a different way. The ancient Greeks held that human existence was determined, among other things, by man's assessment of his own possibilities. Hopes were subjective expectations about one's own future. They had no basis in reality.

According to legend the god Zeus gave man a container full of good things. Man, curious animal that he is, lifted the lid to peek inside and all the good things escaped to the gods—only hope was trapped inside and is all that man now has. And even hope is a mixed blessing. Only a god realizes all his expectations; man's hopes are always uncertain. It was Euripides, the fourth-century B.C. tragic dramatist, who said, "Where there is life there is hope," but that was simply a statement of fact, not an encouragement about the future. Hope has no element of security— it merely projects the future.

Hope, in the New Testament, is quite different. It is not a fragile expectation about an uncertain future but the confident anticipation of what will certainly come to pass. It is based not upon human projections but upon divine declaration. It is the joyous realization that God has determined the course of all future history. He has decided what the future will be. For this reason "hope does not disappoint us" (v. 5). It will not put us to shame by turning out to be an illusion.

Christian hope is based squarely upon the character of God Himself. For the believer the future holds the remarkable prospect of "sharing the glory of God" (5:2, *Goodspeed*). The radiance of God's presence will become the adornment of God's children. "When he appears, we shall be like him" (1 John 3:2).

In another place Paul speaks of a mystery "which is Christ in you, the hope of glory" (Col. 1:27). Our hope of sharing God's glory is based squarely upon the reality of Christ's indwelling presence. He is the guarantee of future glory. No uncertainty here! Similarly, in 1 Timothy 1:1, "Christ Jesus [is] our hope." Outside of Christ men are "without hope and without God in the world" (Eph. 2:12) but we have been given "new birth into a living hope through the resurrection of Jesus Christ from the dead" (1 Pet. 1:3).

Much more could be written about the hope of the redeemed, but this brief sketch is enough to make us realize the tremendous gulf between the hope[lessness] of natural man and the hope of believers. For one the future is uncertain, a plaything in the hands of whatever gods may be. For the other the future is sure. In this future, it is determined that the believer will share in the glory of God. Small wonder that "we rejoice in . . . hope!"

We Rejoice in God

"We rejoice in the hope of the glory of God" (Rom. 5:2). "We also rejoice in our sufferings" (v. 3). "We also rejoice in God through our Lord Jesus Christ" (v. 11).

It is significant that three times in verses 1-11 of Romans 5 Paul speaks of rejoicing. Joy is most certainly one of the major benefits of believing. A word or two about the Greek word for "rejoice" in the three verses just cited. The *Authorized King James* version translates "rejoice" in verse 2, "glory" in verse 3, and "joy" in verse 11. The word is *kauchaomai*, to boast about or to take pride in. It can be used in a negative sense to mean self-glorification. To a braggart we might say, "Quit boasting about how good you are!" Paul uses the term in a different sense. The boasting of the Christian has nothing to do with his own accomplishments. It boasts in what *God* has done. In this context "boasting" denotes exultation and rejoicing based upon the character and saving activity of God. As Paul quotes in 1 Corinthians 1:31, "Let him who boasts boast in the Lord." Let your joy break forth because of what God has done to free you from the guilt and power of sin.

Believers rejoice first of all in the confident expecta-

tion of sharing in the divine glory (see v. 2). This true destiny of man was lost through sin but regained by the death of Christ. Upon His triumphal return at the end of the age, the restoration of divine radiance will be complete. This theme was discussed in the previous section.

Secondly, believers rejoice in their sufferings (see v. 3). This is not an exhortation to rejoice in the midst of hardships but a declaration that the justified do in fact rejoice because of their suffering. And why do afflictions provide the basis for rejoicing? Because they are evidence that God is leading us along the path toward spiritual maturity. As the author of Hebrews puts it, "If you are not disciplined . . . then you are illegitimate children and not true sons. . . . God disciplines us for our good, that we may share in his holiness" (Heb. 12:8,10). The reason why we "rejoice in our sufferings" is because "suffering produces perseverance; perseverance, character; and character, hope" (Rom. 5:3,4). James 1:2 emphasizes the same point. Overcoming as a Christian means taking the obstacle itself which was placed in our way and using it as a basis for greater achievement. Instead of falling over it we use it as a stepping stone.

Finally, in verse 11, we read that believers "rejoice in God through our Lord Jesus Christ." God Himself is the ultimate cause for joy. God is joy as much as He is love. Our imperfect perceptions of God often lead us to see Him as an inordinately serious Ruler of the universe who has very little to rejoice about, given man's continuing penchant for sin. Jesus tells His disciples to remain in His love "so that my joy may be in you and that your joy may be complete" (John 15:11). God's presence is the place of perfect joy. Sorrow is a result of sin. When sin is forever put away only joy will remain. This is why we now "rejoice in God."

We Have God's Love

"God has poured out his love into our hearts by the Holy Spirit, whom he has given us" (Rom. 5:5). Another major benefit of believing is the full assurance that we are the recipients of God's love. God pours out His love into our hearts. He enables us by His Holy Spirit to grasp at the very center of our being the fullness of His love. Elsewhere Paul prays that we may know "how wide and long and high and deep is the love of Christ" (Eph. 3:18). To be loved is one thing; to comprehend the dimensions of that love is something quite distinct. To the Corinthians Paul writes that those things which God has prepared for those who love Him—which "no eye has seen, no ear has heard, no mind has conceived"—have been "revealed . . . to us by his Spirit" (1 Cor. 2:9,10).

The distinctive thing about God's love is that it stems entirely from the character of God Himself. It is in no sense a response to any worth in its object. God does not love man because man is lovable. Human love flourishes as a response to love received. Not so, God's love. Because it is self-caused it can be freely given. Most readers have been told of the three Greek words for love. *Eros* (according to A. M. Hunter) is all take; *philia* is give and take; *agapē* is all give. God's love is *agapē*.

Romans 5:6-8 prove beyond doubt that God loves sinners just as they are. *Poor Richard's Almanac* says that "God helps them that help themselves." Paul says that God helps those who *cannot help themselves* ("When we were still powerless, Christ died for the ungodly"; (Rom. 5:6). The powerlessness (or weakness) of which the apostle speaks is the moral inability to meet the righteous demands of God. Natural man is ungodly, not in the sense that he is as grossly wicked as he might be; he is ungodly in the sense that having rebelled against his Creator he is without God. Separated from God he is ungodly; that is, he is lost. This is why "Christ died for the ungodly." By means of His sacrificial death He opened a way of return for all who believe.

The fact that Christ died for us, the ungodly, is central to New Testament theology (see for example Mark 14:24; 2 Cor. 5:21; Titus 2:14). The death of Christ is the ultimate proof of God's love. A love that does not act is no more than an abstraction. "God so loved that he *gave*" (see John 3:16).

Romans 5:7 stresses the uniqueness of Christ's act of love. It is a rare thing for a man to lay down his life even for a righteous man. Only slightly less unusual would it be for a person to lay down his life for a "good man" (the word is expanded in the *Amplified New Testament* to designate "a noble and lovable and generous benefactor"). The amazing thing is that in view of man's understandable reticence to die for the just and honorable, Christ died *for the ungodly*. "While we were still sinners, Christ died for us"—a most remarkable demonstration of divine love (v. 8).

Deliverance from Wrath

"Since we have now been justified by his blood, how much more shall we be saved from God's wrath through him!" (v. 9).

This form of reasoning is called the argument from the greater to the lesser. Since God has done the more difficult task (He justified the ungodly), we may be confident that He is well able to do that which by comparison is much easier (deliver from the coming wrath those who believe).

In chapter 1 Paul taught that in the gospel there is revealed not only the righteousness of God but also His wrath. This wrath will be visited upon all unrighteousness. If this were not so God would not be a righteous God. In a moral universe God must necessarily oppose all that is contrary to His righteous nature. God's wrath is merely the negative expression of His holiness. Without hatred of evil, holiness loses its meaning.

Paul and the people of his time understood the reality of divine wrath. They had not been led astray by the well-intentioned but misguided idea that God's love cancelled out His wrath. To be saved from wrath was a highly meaningful and personal truth. It was bound to be included in any list of the benefits of believing.

Reconciliation

"For if, when we were God's enemies, we were reconciled to him . . . how much more, having been reconciled, shall we be saved through his life!" (Rom. 5:10).

It is interesting to note that the idea of reconciliation played no significant role in the Greco-Roman religions of Paul's day. To be reconciled means to be brought back into a friendly relationship with someone. It assumes prior separation, a state of previous hostility. Reconciliation is a personal matter. For this reason it was essentially missing in first-century pagan religion. Men and their gods were not related in any intimate way.

At the heart of the Christian faith lies a personal relationship. To believe in Christ is not to subscribe to a set of theological affirmations; it is to trust in a person— Jesus Christ, the Son of God, who died for my sins, rose again from the grave and now lives in a real and personal way in my heart. By His death and resurrection He reconciled man to Himself. That is, He removed the enmity which came as a result of human sin.

Christ opened the way for man to return to God's favor and friendship. Reconciliation is complete when man by faith takes this crucial step of faith.

Nowhere are the two steps of reconciliation better expressed than in Paul's second letter to the Corinthians. It is through Christ that God "reconciled us to himself" (2 Cor. 5:18). This is what He has done; therefore we implore you on His behalf, "Be reconciled to God" (v. 20). This is what we "do." God has reconciled but we must "be reconciled" ("Make your peace with God" is *Phillips'* rendering of the imperative).

These, then, are the benefits of believing—the blessings that come to the person of faith as a result of his right-standing before God. He has *peace* with God, *access* to His royal presence, *hope* of sharing the divine splendor, a solid basis for *rejoicing*, the *love* of God poured out into his heart, *deliverance from wrath*, and *reconciliation to our heavenly Father*. In His gracc God has forgiven the past, made the present bright with promise, and holds out an even more glorious future.

For Discussion

Have you ever noticed that spiritual truth requires a bit of thought and meditation before it begins to grip the imagination and stir the fires of devotion? Its transforming power is released only to those who demonstrate their desire by opening themselves prayerfully to what it has to say. This takes time and the decision to pay the price of spiritual discipline.

Chapter 5 of Romans is rich with life-changing truth. It is not available, however, to the casual reader. What has been your own experience as you've studied these 11 verses? Has the reality of God's peace and love come home to you with greater force? Is it important to you on a personal basis that by Christ's death you have been reconciled to God? How would you recommend that this section be studied so that its truth will make a lasting impact on your life? Do you think it would be helpful to go back over the seven benefits of believing and spend whatever time is necessary in order to allow God's Spirit the opportunity to make each concept as vividly relevant as possible? If so, will you do it?

Does Justification by Faith Lead to Sin?

Romans 6:1-25

Romans 1-4 settled beyond the shadow of a doubt the essential truth of the gospel, that is, that man is saved by faith alone totally apart from any meritorious activity on his own part. Salvation is the free gift of God. The only way to receive it is to accept it for what it is—an expression of God's unmerited favor toward those who believe.

This doctrine presented a severe stumbling block to the Jew. Had not God Himself given the laws and commandments to the Hebrew people? Were they not expressions of the divine intent for man? Did they not regulate with at least some success the conduct of God's people? What would happen if suddenly the law were removed? Would not chaos follow? Certainly, any teaching which would displace the central role of law would do so at the expense of righteousness.

Paul was fully aware that questions like these would be raised. In the latter part of chapter 5 he stated that "the law was added so that the trespass might increase" (5:20)—a point of view thoroughly unacceptable to a Jewish audience. "But where sin increased," Paul continued, "grace increased all the more" (5:20). It would appear that Paul has fallen into a trap of his own making. If increased sin demonstrates more fully the extent of God's grace, then sin is a good thing after all. The more we sin the more God's grace is magnified! And doesn't this very statement expose the corrupt nature of Paul's doctrine? Can anyone logically take the position that God's cause in the world is helped along by sin?

Shall We Sin in Order to Magnify the Grace of God?

Chapter 6 is structured around two basic questions which Paul's opponents were sure to ask. The questions are not asked out of any real desire to know the truth. They are intended to point out the unacceptable implications which from the detractors' point of view must necessarily follow from Paul's basic premise. They are designed to refute the doctrine of justification by faith alone.

The first question is, "Shall we go on sinning so that grace may increase?" (v. 1). Paul's immediate response is, "By no means!" (v. 2). The entire idea is absurd. Why? Because everyone who has been justified by faith has "died to sin." We have been separated from sin by death. Sin belongs on the other side of the grave. This being true, Paul asks the obvious question, "How can we live in it any longer?" (v. 2).

It is not difficult to understand on a theoretical basis that we have died to sin. In Christ the payment for our sins was made. He died for our sins. They have no further claim on us. Yet from a practical point of view, we, more often than we wish, find ourselves guilty of sinning (see 7:14-23). It seems as if we are caught in a basic dilemma. In Christ we died to sin yet in fact sin has by no means died to us! Let's trace the argument as it develops in the following verses.

In verses 3 and 4 Paul reminds his readers that to be baptized into Christ means to become one with Him in His death and burial. The only point of contact that a sinner can have with Christ is at the point of Christ's death. The cross alone spans the chasm from man's sin to God's forgiveness. All who come to God come by way of the cross. The expression, "baptized into Christ," means to become one with Him, to be incorporated into His fellowship. Elsewhere Paul writes in a similar vein of the Israelites who were "baptized into Moses" (1 Cor. 10:2). The verb is used in a metaphorical sense.

The important point is that when we were incorporated into Christ we joined in His death. His death for sin became our death to the claims of sin. If we are not one with Him in His death we remain unforgiven. Only in Christ has there been atonement for sin.

It is helpful to remember that Paul is drawing out a relationship between the actual death of Christ for sin and our "death" to sin as that power which has controlled our life. We are dealing with an analogy and all analogies break down when pressed beyond a certain point. Cranfield, in his splendid commentary on Romans, points out four quite different senses in which Christians are said to have died to sin: juridical, baptismal, moral, eschatological. While this involves a sophistication beyond our present needs, it does underscore the fact that Paul is making his point by the use of a relevant analogy and that to press his words directly into a theological formulation would be to misconstrue his intent.

Our union with Christ in His death is only part of the story. As He was raised from the dead in a glorious manifestation of the power of God so also do we share His resurrection in the sense that we are raised to an entirely new kind of life. This "life after death" has no obligation to sin. It is free from the power of sin. It is life shared with Christ (see Rom. 6:8). It is being alive to God (see v. 11).

Verses 5-10 expand the same line of thought. As any

good teacher knows it is not enough to state a truth once and expect it to be fully grasped. What Paul is writing is so important that it calls for restatement and enlargement. If we have become one with Christ by sharing in His death—and we have!—it follows that we will be united with Him in a resurrection like His (see v. 5). At this point Paul is not discussing our bodily resurrection. That will take place at the appropriate time. What he is saying is that as our death was a death to sin, so will our resurrection be a resurrection to a new kind of life. Christ's actual death and resurrection serve as a pattern for our death to sin and resurrection to new life.

It is clear that our old self ("the man we once were," *NEB*) was put to death with Christ so that the body of sin (that is, the body as the instrument of carnality) would become powerless and henceforth we would no longer be in bondage to evil (see v. 6). Our old self is what we were when under the control of sin. The "old man" (or sinful nature) is not some segment of our person which can be removed and replaced by a "new man." It is not a damaged module which affects the entire machine. Our old man is the person we were when dominated by the power of sin. But when we died in Christ this old self was stripped of its capacity to control. We are no longer its slaves. Because we have died to sin we are immune from its power (see v. 7).

To change the figure, sin was conquered by the death of Christ; it exists at the present time as a defeated foe. The man in Christ need not yield to its desires; although it is still around and intent on establishing its fraudulent claims, it remains in fact a defeated enemy. Whatever authority it exercises over believers it has received from their unwitting acceptance of its blustering pretensions. To be freed from sin does not mean to be released from any tendency to do wrong. Honesty compels us to admit that we know of no such release. The writings of our greatest saints testify to the fact that sin continues to harass the believer with its devious approaches and subtle temptations. We are freed from sin in the sense that our death in Christ sets us free from the consequences of sin and from the obligation to yield to its demand. We need not go down in defeat.

Having shared thus in the death of Christ we are convinced that we shall also share in His life (see v. 8). In that Christ was raised from the dead and cannot die again, "death no longer has mastery over him" (see v. 9). In that He died to sin once for all, He now "lives forever in unbroken fellowship with God" (v. 10, *Taylor*). For us to share in this new life is to live free of sin's control in the presence of God. Although His relationship to sin is absolute, and therefore differs from ours, it does provide a pattern and example of how we are to live. The power to live this new life will be discussed in the following chapter.

Verses 11-14 draw out the practical implications of our union with Christ in His death and resurrection. "In the same way," writes Paul, "count yourselves dead to sin but alive to God in Christ Jesus" (v. 11). *Phillips* translates, "In the same way look upon yourselves as dead to the appeal and power of sin but alive and sensitive to the call of God." We are not called upon to *pretend* that we are dead to sin. Paul is not advocating the power of positive thinking. Nor are we to look upon this injunction as an ideal toward which we should aspire, knowing in reality that it can never be achieved. The Greek word translated "count" depicts a deliberate and sober judgment. In context this judgment is based upon the gospel. Since the gospel declares that you died in Christ and have risen to a new quality of life, consider it to be true and act accordingly.

Christianity is a way of life. Believers in the early church were called people of the Way (see Acts 9:2; 24:22). It is eminently practical. "Therefore do not let sin reign in your mortal body so that you obey its evil desires" (Rom. 6:12). Paul's entire discourse is directed toward this end. The original suggestion was, Why not go on sinning so as to magnify the grace of God? (see v. 1). Paul can now answer with a straightforward, "Don't allow sin to go on lording it over you. Don't offer any part of your body to be used as an instrument of wickedness. Rather, put yourselves at God's disposal as men who have been brought back from death to life. Devote all your human faculties to the cause of righteousness" (see v. 13). The Christian is pictured as a warrior brought back to life. He is to choose whether to offer his "weapons" (the same word as in 2 Cor. 10:4: "the weapons we fight with are not the weapons of the world") to Sin or to Righteousness. Sin was his former master and led him toward death. Righteousness is his new master and leads to life. To claim that one follows Righteousness and yet continues to serve Sin would be rank treason! In any other setting such an act of betrayal would be worthy of disgrace and death.

Sin shall not continue to control the Christian. It shall exercise no authority over you. Why? Because you are no longer under the jurisdiction and control of the law but are governed by the unmerited favor of God (see Rom. 6:14). Your only obligation is to grace. Sin is no longer your master. You need not respond to the promptings of the old self. What you were has been stripped of its power by your decision to believe in Christ. Your faith has brought about a supernatural transformation in your reigning affections. The new self responds to the grace of God. It is obedient to the promptings of righteousness. Count it to be so and stop lending your powers to the enemy who once held you firmly in his grasp.

Shall We Sin Because We're No Longer Under Law?

Paul's statement that those who are justified by faith are no longer "under law, but under grace" (v. 14) provided another opportunity for his opponents to press home what they thought to be a logical implication of the doctrine. "What then? Shall we sin because we are not under law but under grace?" (v. 15). The idea that it doesn't make any difference whether a believer sins or not, since he is no longer under law, is central to a heresy commonly called antinomianism. The term is compounded from *anti* ("against" in the sense of pursuing an opposite policy) and *nomos* (law). The antinomian believed that since he was no longer obliged to keep the law he was free to do whatever he wished. Since God's forgiveness was an expression of unmerited favor it made no difference how the one receiving that forgiveness would conduct his life. The antinomian reasoned that since he was free from law and under grace he had a license to sin as much as he wanted to.

Paul answers, "By no means!" (v. 15). This short phrase or one similar, occurs repeatedly in Romans (3:4,6,31; 6:2,15; 7:7,13; 9:14; 11:1,11) and elsewhere throughout Paul's letters. Translators have enjoyed coming up with new ways of representing the original: "Of course not!" (*Phillips*). "Never!" (*Moffatt*). "Heaven forbid!" (*TCNT*). Paul's extensive use of the phrase reveals something of the personality of the apostle and his style in defending the faith against those who would twist it to their own ends.

Note, however, that being "under grace" does not mean to be free from all obligation. What the Christian is free from is the enslaving power of the law. Law entered the picture in order that men might become conscious of sin (see 3:20). Paul even goes so far as to say that "the law was added so that the trespass might increase" (5:20). The role of the law was to make specific the sinfulness of man. In Romans 7 the apostle writes that he "would not have known what sin was except through the law" (v. 7). The law itself is holy (see 7:12) but its effect is to bring into bold relief the sinful nature of man. It prepares the way for salvation by grace. It brings the repentant sinner to his knees and causes him to rely completely upon the mercy of God.

Thus it does not follow that once the condemnation of the law has been removed a person is free to do whatever he wants. In another place Paul writes that in ministering to the Gentiles he became like one "not having the law." He recognized, however, that he was not free from divine obligation but remained "under Christ's law" (1 Cor. 9:21). In Romans he arrives at the same conclusion but argues along a slightly different line. From the general principle that everyone is a slave to whomever he obeys, Paul reasons that while man has the option of serving either Sin or Righteousness, he does not have the option of serving neither. Thus to be under grace does not remove a person from the obligations of divine favor.

This general principle is spelled out in Romans 6:16. "You surely know, do you not, that you are slaves to the one you obey, either to Sin which results in death or to Obedience which leads to righteousness?" (paraphrased). In the sight of God these are the only options. A person either obeys or disobeys. He must choose either Sin or Righteousness. Whatever his choice he remains a slave.

Paul hurries on to thank God that although his readers had formerly been slaves to sin they had wholeheartedly taken a new master. They "obeyed the form of teaching to which [they] were entrusted" (v. 17). This interesting expression provides insight into the role of Christian doctrine in the early church. New converts were placed under an accepted standard of doctrine. Jewish rabbis thought of themselves as masters of their tradition. They created and controlled the material that grew up around the Mosaic law. Christians, on the other hand, were created by the Word of God and must remain in obedience to it. Peter writes to his fellow believers that they had been born again "by God's living and enduring word" (1 Pet. 1:23, *Weymouth*). Luke speaks of his sources as eyewitnesses and "servants of the word" (Luke 1:2). The church of Jesus Christ has always remained strong and virile when it has been willing to place itself in subjection to the Word of God.

Continuing his remarks to the Christians at Rome Paul writes, "You have been set free from sin and have become slaves to righteousness" (6:18). There is no way that anyone can claim that being free from the law provides opportunity for sin. In essence, what a believer has done is to change masters. He has not exchanged bondage for some mythical freedom from all restraint. The old restraint was oppressive and led to death. The new restraint is positive and guides toward life. One blocked the entrance to divine favor; the other results from having received that favor. One was an obligation to perform in order to be accepted; the other an obligation to live in harmony with the One who has already accepted you. Both law and grace have their origin in God but only grace can justify the ungodly. Legalists tried to twist law into a method of extracting God's favor. In so doing they simply revealed the extent to which sin had perverted their under-standing of true righteousness.

In striving for clarity Paul used by way of illustration the practice of slavery. To compare obedience to God with slavery could be misinterpreted, so he adds, "I use an everyday illustration because human nature grasps truth more readily that way" (v. 19, *Phillips*; a rather loose but helpful paraphrase). Analogies are intended to throw light on a subject by comparing it with something else which is more fully known. What is sometimes forgotten is the obvious fact that without differences there could be no analogy. Interpreters must resist the tendency to press similarities beyond that which is intended. For example, while it is proper to understand our obedience to God as a form of "slavery," it would be improper to read back into the relationship everything that could be said about the institution of slavery. God, for instance, is not a slave driver nor are we His bootblacks.

Verses 19b-23 resume the practical thrust of verses 12, 13 and extend the application. As you once offered every part of your body to impurity and ever-increasing wickedness, now surrender them to the service of righteousness with sanctification as a goal (see v. 19). Sanctification (as the form of the Greek word indicates) is to be understood in terms of a process rather than a state. It is more in keeping with the teaching of the New Testament to say that obedient Christians are *being sanctified* than to say they *are* sanctified. Sanctification is a process by which we are being changed from what we were to what we ultimately are to be. It is being "conformed to the likeness of [God's] Son" (Rom. 8:29). By offering all our human faculties as slaves to righteousness we experience ethical and spiritual renewal. The goal of sanctification is to become like Jesus Christ.

Paul reminds his readers that when they were slaves to sin they "were free from the control of righteousness" (6:20). But what did you get out of it? Nothing except those things of which you are now ashamed. In the long run they spell death (see v. 21). But now you are free from the bondage of sin. You have entered the service of God and reap the benefits of being on the road to holiness. The end result of that is "eternal life" (v. 22). Two masters and two destinies: slavery to Sin which leads to eternal separation from God (death), and slavery to Righteousness which leads to eternal life. In Elijah's words, "How long will you waver between two opinions? If the Lord is God, follow him; but if Baal is God, follow him" (1 Kings 18:21). Or in Joshua's words, "Choose for yourselves this day whom you will serve" (Josh. 24:15).

Paul draws his argument to a close with yet another comparison: "The wages of sin is death, but the gift of God is eternal life" (Rom. 6:23). The couplet contains two military words. The word translated "wages" was used for a soldier's daily pay. John the Baptist answered the soldiers' inquiry about what they should do, with the exhortation, "Don't extort money" or accuse falsely and "be content with your pay" (Luke 3:14, same word). In contrast, the word "gift" was used for a bounty distributed to the army on special occasions such as the accession of a new emperor to the throne. (In Latin it was called a *donativum*.) Thus, Sin pays wages to its servants, and what one earns is death. Not so, God; He distributes free gifts to those who will accept and His gift is eternal life. By sinning we earned death; by faith we receive life. And this life comes through union with Christ Jesus our Lord.

For Discussion

I once knew a person who said that he intended to have

a good time on earth and take a backseat in heaven. He had it all figured out. Why not get the best out of both worlds? By "believing" he would be assured of a place in heaven. By not committing himself to a righteous life he would get the most out of the time he put in on earth.

What's wrong with this idea? Is this a modern example of antinomianism? Why do you suppose anyone would believe that it doesn't make any difference how a Christian lives? Is there any support in Scripture for this doctrine? Do you accept the saying, "If He isn't Lord of · all, He isn't Lord at all"?

What about carnal Christians? Can a person decide to be carnal and still make it into heaven? Does God allow the believer to choose between two options—spiritual or carnal? How would you go about using chapter 6 of Romans to show that believers are still under obligation to the "law of Christ"? List several examples of antinomian tendencies in the contemporary church.

7

Life in the Spirit

For most Christians the eighth chapter of Romans is a high point in New Testament revelation. Along with Matthew 5-7 (the Sermon on the Mount) and 1 Corinthians 13 (the centrality of love) it provides extraordinary inspiration and spiritual insight.

The Greek word for "spirit" occurs 34 times in the book of Romans. Twenty-one of these are to be found in a single chapter of the book. Chapter 8 is supremely the chapter of the Spirit. In only two of the 21 references does the term clearly refer to something other than the Holy Spirit.

In Romans 8 Paul presents his doctrine of the Holy Spirit; yet his purpose at this point is not to tell us about the person of the Holy Spirit (and His relationship to the two other members of the trinity). It is, rather, to spell out the role of the Spirit in His relationship to the life of the believer. Thus we have named the first half of the chapter, *Life in the Spirit* (vv. 1-17), and the second half, *The Triumph of Believing* (vv. 18-39). The entire chapter is built around the work of the Spirit. For example, He controls the believer (see v. 6), causes him to cry, "*Abba*, Father" (v. 15), "helps us in our weakness" (v. 26), "intercedes" for us (v. 27). To grasp Paul's teaching on the Spirit is to understand the secret of living victoriously while surrounded by sin and impaired by human frailty. How to live in and by the Spirit is the single most important lesson the believer can ever learn.

No Condemnation

Romans 8 opens with one of the most joyous declarations to be found anywhere in the New Testament: "Therefore, there is now no condemnation for those who are in Christ Jesus." Scholars point out that the "therefore" points back to 7:6 with its proclamation that "we have been released from the law" (the intervening verses, 7-25, clarify the role of law). Since we have been set free from the obligations of the law we are no longer under its condemnation. "Now" means ever since the death and resurrection of Christ. By His death He fulfilled the righteous demands of the law. Those who are "in Christ Jesus" share His freedom from the obligations of the law.

The condemnation of which Paul speaks is an objective fact. Law led to sin (see 5:13) and sin to judgment (see 5:16). The commandment which was intended to bring life "actually brought death" (7:10). It is primarily this objective condemnation which is done away with in Christ.

Man, however, is also burdened with a sense of condemnation, guilt over past sins and an apparent inability to live the Christian life more successfully. Most Christians are plagued by psychological guilt. They find themselves caught in the Romans 7 predicament—"I have the desire to do what is good, but I cannot carry it out. For what I do is not the good I want to do; no, the evil I do not want to do—this I keep on doing" (vv. 18,19). Even when God Himself assures them in Scripture that they are forgiven (see 1 John 1:9) they find themselves unable to accept forgiveness in any sort of real and personal way.

They labor through life under the burden of self-imposed psychological guilt. But if God has removed the actual cause of our guilt (and He has) we do Him a disservice when we punish ourselves with guilt *feelings*. Romans 8:1 tells us not only that the condemnation of the law (objective guilt) has been removed but also that all our subjective guilt has no further basis in reality. In Christ we have been "born [again] free."

Verse 2 speaks of two laws. One is the law of sin and death, that is, the principle that sin leads to death (*Phillips* calls it, "the old vicious circle of sin and death"). The other is the principle of life by the Spirit (A.M. Hunter understands the compound phrase to mean, "the law of the Spirit, that is, life in Christ Jesus"). More simply, to be controlled by sin means death; to be controlled by the Spirit means life.

Verses 3 and 4 explain how the "law of the Spirit" sets the believer free from the "law of sin." The Mosaic Law was not able to accomplish its goal because man's sinful nature robbed it of its power. There was nothing wrong with the Law itself. It was our own human nature that undermined the Law and thwarted its design. But what the Law could not do God did by sending His Son "in the likeness of sinful man to be a sin offering." This clause requires explanation. What does it mean that Christ was in the "likeness of sinful man"? It obviously does not mean that He was a sinner (see 2 Cor. 5:21). Nor does it mean that He was made to *appear* as a sinful man (while remaining sinless). What it does mean is that Jesus took upon Himself the nature of man with all its human tendencies. It was as man that He lived a sinless life. He was "tempted in every way, just as we are—yet was without sin" (Heb. 4:15). By His life He fulfilled the righteous demands of the law. His obedience becomes our obedience. As the unblemished Lamb of God He fulfilled His mission by giving Himself as "a sin offering" (Rom. 8:3).

God passed judgment on sin so that the righteous requirements of the law might be fully met in our case (see v. 4). He signed the death warrant for sin in order that we would be able to break free from the control of our sinful nature and allow the Spirit to control our life—thus fulfilling the original intention of law. While it is true that the law's demands have been met by the sinless life of Christ, more needs to be said. The significance of this great redemptive act for the lives of believers needs to be stressed. Because the power of sin was condemned by Christ's perfect obedience we have been given the Spirit and empowered to live in such a way that the quality of life prescribed by law is fulfilled in our daily experience. In Christ we are righteous. By walking in the Spirit we become what we already are in Christ.

Who's in Control?

In the final analysis there are only two ways to live. A person may follow the dictates of his fallen nature or the promptings of the Spirit. Apart from Christ, man is controlled by his human nature. He thinks and acts in a way that is consistent with what he is—a member of the human family. Paul writes, "Those who live according to the sinful nature have their minds set on what that nature desires" (v. 5). To set one's mind on something involves a definite act of the will. Paul uses the same word in Philippians 3:19 where, in speaking of the "enemies of the cross of Christ," he says, "They are absorbed in earthly matters" (*Goodspeed*). They have decided to give their full attention to that which belongs to life apart from God. Their entire thought life is controlled by their lower nature.

But there is another way of living. Those who belong to Christ allow the Spirit to control all they do. Their minds are "set on what the Spirit desires" (Rom. 8:5). They are led by the Spirit. They give their attention to those things which are spiritual—that is, which are consistent with and prompted by the indwelling Spirit.

Note that both sinful human nature and the Holy Spirit have desires; there is something each wishes to accomplish. The basic problem faced by the child of God is that although the Spirit of God has taken up residence in his life, the old nature has not been removed. Thus a conflict is set up between the old man (what he was when dominated by his sinful nature) and the new man (what he is becoming as he lives under the control of the Spirit). Whenever a Christian allows his sinful nature to control his life in any way he is taking sides with the enemy. Sin is treason. It is forsaking God to serve the enemy.

Destiny is determined by the set of the mind. The mind-set of sinful man is death. Following the impulses of a fallen and sinful nature leads to death. But the mind which is controlled by the Spirit results in life and peace. It should be perfectly clear that what we are now becoming determines what we will be. That is axiomatic. To give our attention to the desires of the sinful nature is to be led toward the predetermined end of all sin, which is death. Revelation speaks of death and Hades being "thrown into the lake of fire" (Rev. 20:14). To give our attention to the desires of the Spirit, however, is to receive joy and peace. One cannot follow the road of sin and expect it to lead to life. Each road leads to a separate destiny.

Verse 7a completes the sentence that began with verse 6 (the *KJV* and a few others put a period after v. 6 and begin a new sentence). "The mind of sinful man is death,

. . . [because] the sinful mind is hostile to God." *Beck*
translates, "This is so because the fleshly mind hates
God." Since God is life, that which stands over against
God must lead to death. It is important to understand the
basic antipathy between man's sinful human nature and
his new nature (which is spiritual) in Christ. The warfare
between the two never ends. Détente is out of the question. How the new man is able to conquer will be taken up
in the following section. For the moment it is important to
understand the essential nature of the conflict.

Paul goes on (in v. 7) to say that the sinful mind "does
not submit to God's law, nor can it do so." Not only does
it refuse to obey the law of God, it is unable to. The ability
to submit to God is not even an option for what the *KJV*
calls "the carnal mind." It is this complete dissimilarity
beween flesh (unredeemed human nature) and Spirit that
accounts for the intensity of the struggle against sin. It
should be perfectly obvious that "those controlled by the
sinful nature cannot please God" (v. 8). To obey the
impulses of the lower nature places a person outside the
favor of God. How could God find pleasure in those who
consort with the enemy? Sin in the life of the believer is
treason. Throughout the Old Testament, idolatry is por-
trayed as spiritual infidelity. Jeremiah reprimands Israel
for her "adulteries and lustful neighings," her "shameless
prostitution" (Jer. 13:27). Old Testament infidelity becomes New Testament treason. The underlying issue is
the same. Sin is serious business. Little wonder that those
whose lives are controlled by the sin-principle are unable
to please God!

The Spirit-Controlled Life

After marking out the clear distinction between those
who follow the dictates of their sinful nature and those

who are led by the Spirit of God, Paul moves quickly ahead to assure his readers that *they* are Spirit controlled: "You, however, are controlled not by the sinful nature but by the Spirit" (Rom. 8:9). To be justified in the sight of God means to have died to sin and therefore set free from its authority and control. The power of the sin-principle was broken by the sinless life of Christ and the giving of Himself as an atonement for sin (see 8:3). Those who are in Christ share in this victory over sin. No longer do they remain in bondage to their sinful nature. A new master has taken over—"the Spirit of God [who] lives in you" (v. 9).

Before salvation, man was controlled by his sinful human nature. After salvation, control was turned over to the Spirit of God. At no time has man been absolutely free to do whatever he wants. He acts in conformity to what he was (fallen and therefore sinful) or to what he has become in Christ (a new man fashioned in righteousness). Autonomous man is a myth. There exists no state of moral neutrality which allows freedom of choice apart from the pressures of sin or the Spirit. The spiritual growth of the believer is in exact proportion to his continuing willingness to yield to the promptings of the Holy Spirit. One might paraphrase the challenge of Elijah, "Choose you this day which life-controlling force you will obey: your sinful nature which leads to death or the indwelling spirit who leads to life" (see 1 Kings 18:21).

The first part of Romans 8:9 teaches that every Christian has the Spirit. The *NIV*'s "if" is better translated "since": You are controlled by the Spirit "since the Spirit of God lives within you" (*TCNT*). The latter part of the verse teaches that anyone without the Spirit does not belong to Christ. This is Scripture's clearest refutation of the idea that Christians may receive the Spirit at a point in time subsequent to their salvation. It is the presence of the

Spirit Himself in the life of a person that makes him a Christian. No Spirit, no saving relationship. Listen closely to verse 9b: "If anyone does not have the Spirit of Christ, he does not belong to Christ."

On the other hand, if Christ is in you, although your body must die because of sin, your spirit is enjoying life because you have a right standing before God (see v. 10). The body will die because it belongs to the realm of the finite which by definition is limited. The spirit (the inner man made alive by the Holy Spirit), however, has been resurrected to new life on the basis of a righteousness provided by the redemptive activity of Christ. Furthermore, if the Spirit of God (who raised Jesus from the dead) has taken possession of you, then this same Spirit will also raise you again at the last day (see v. 11).

Obviously it is God who gives life. He gives it, however, through His Spirit. Verse 11 says, in effect, that since you have the Spirit of God, and since God raised Jesus from the dead, you may be sure that God will also raise you by means of the same Spirit. Our hope of future resurrection rests upon the indwelling presence of God's life-giving Spirit.

(Many commentaries begin a new section with verse 12. The following verses set forth the practical conclusion which may be drawn from verses 1-11. The subject of verses 12 and 13, however, is the same as the preceding paragraph and verse 14 marks the transition into a new section dealing with believers as sons of God and coheirs with Christ. Thus we divide between verses 13 and 14.)

"Therefore, brothers, we have an obligation" (v. 12). Because we are under the Spirit's control we are responsible to carry out His wishes. Our obligation is certainly "not to the sinful nature, to live according to it" (v. 12). We owe nothing to the old nature. Our relationship to what we were ended with death. Its "obligations" were paid in full by the death of Christ. We are free from its demands. Living according to the sinful nature ends appropriately in death. But if by virtue of our new relationship to the Spirit we put to death the evil habits of the old man, we "will live" (v. 13). Some have taken "if by the Spirit you put to death the misdeeds of the body" to mean that the Christian is armed with the Spirit which he wields as a great weapon in his battle against the evil tendencies of the flesh. A less dramatic (but more accurate) interpretation is that because we are in Christ (and therefore the Spirit is in us) we are empowered to "put an end [to] the evil habits of the body" (*TCNT*). Our obligation is to the Spirit. By turning over control to Him we put a stop to all the evil tendencies which flow from our sinful natures.

Christians face the awkward and discomforting problem of a dual nature. We are in a sense morally schizophrenic. One nature is fallen and therefore sinful. The other nature is new and desires righteousness. Elsewhere Paul speaks of this new nature as "created to be like God in true righteousness and holiness" (Eph. 4:24). Both natures compete for control. They are not, however, equally powerful. The old nature is deceitful and tries to gain control through subterfuge and illicit appeal. The new nature will always win out whenever we allow it to take over. Our role in this struggle is to say no to the intrigues of the old nature and yes to the promise of the new.

Someone explained it this way. Inside of me are two dogs. They are always fighting. Should you ask me which one wins I would have to confess, "The one I feed the most." An analogy, of course, yet in our struggle against sin is it not true that when we feed our old nature it wins the day, but when we say yes to the indwelling Spirit does He not always win the skirmish?

Sons of God and Coheirs with Christ

It has been argued by some that every person in the world is a child of God. Did not God create all mankind? John 1:9 with its declaration that Christ is the true light "which enlightens every man coming into the world" (*TCNT*) is often quoted in support. This argument is answered a few verses later where John goes on to say that when Christ came into His own creation His own people did not receive Him, but to those who did receive Him He gave the right "to become children of God" (John 1:11,12). Man is not a child of God because he is part of the human race. Only those who are born into God's family (by receiving Christ) can claim Him as Father.

While this teaching is quite clear, there remains some question about what it means to receive Christ. Some propose that it means to accept His deity as a valid intellectual proposition. Others think of it as an emotional experience which they equate with conversion. Still others apparently believe that it is possible to receive Christ yet continue to live as one pleases.

The best definition I know of what it means to be a child of God is found in Romans 8:14: "Those who are led by the Spirit of God are sons of God." The nuance of the Greek text is expressed more exactly in *Conybeare* translation, "For all who are led by God's Spirit, and they alone, are the sons of God." To be a son of God one must be continually led (the verb is present tense and denotes an ongoing action) by God's Spirit. It follows that those who are not allowing the Spirit of God to lead them are not His sons.

This understanding of what it means to be a son of

God has profound implications. Our sonship is expressed in the way we live. If we are God's sons we will be Spirit-led. If we are not Spirit-led we don't belong to His family. There is no category of sonship which allows for self-direction. If we follow our old nature we are simply showing that we are still children of Satan (see John 8:44: "You belong to your father, the devil, and you want to carry out your father's desire"). A true son inevitably reflects his father. Sin reveals a filial relationship to Satan; obedience to God's leading is proof that we belong to Him. Are you led by His Spirit? Then you are His son!

Romans 8:15 contrasts two spirits: the spirit of bondage that leads back into fear, and the Spirit of adoption that enables us to call out to God as father. The comparison is between the cringing and fearful demeanor of a slave and the joyful realization of sonship on the part of a child just adopted. In the Greco-Roman world an adopted son received the full benefits and rights of a naturally born son. The act of adoption cancelled all previous obligations and made the child a legal heir of his new father's estate. When we by faith are adopted into God's family all our past debt to sin is cancelled. We become children of a new Father and rightful heirs to all He possesses.

The expression "*Abba*, Father" is important. *Abba* is the Aramaic word for father. It is the term Jesus used in the Garden of Gethsemane when He prayed that the cup of judgment be taken from Him (see Mark 14:36). It reflects the intimate relationship between Jesus and God, His Father. In the ancient Aramaic-speaking world children addressed their father as *Abba*. The ease of pronunciation made it an early and favorite word of young children. It is the Spirit of adoption that enables us to say to God *Abba*, Father. In childlike openness we approach Him not in fear but with the full assurance that we belong to Him and that our presence brings Him joy. It is God's Spirit Himself that "endorses our inward conviction" (*Phillips*) "that we are God's children" (v. 16). In the Old Testament the truth of any statement was established by two witnesses. For the child of God these witnesses are his inward conviction (his "spirit") and the Holy Spirit. When these two agree, we can know that we have been adopted into the family of God.

It follows that "if we are [God's] children, then we are [also His] heirs" (v. 17). There are no second-class sons in the family of God. Our adoption entitles us to all that God has for us. We are heirs of God, and coheirs with Christ. He is our elder brother (see Heb. 2:11-13). We share with Him in the eternal inheritance of joy.

The final clause of verse 17 does not mean that we will be coheirs with Christ on the condition that we suffer with Him. What Paul is saying is that since we share in His sufferings we will also share in His glory. Suffering precedes glory. Montgomery turns the statement around in order to prepare the reader for what will follow in the next paragraph. She translates, "But to share his glory, we must now be sharing his sufferings."

For Discussion

Considerable emphasis has been given to the fact that to be a son of God one must be led by His Spirit. It is the presence and activity of God's Spirit in the life of the believer that testifies to the fact that he is a child of God.

The serious question then arises, What must be said about such a large segment of the contemporary Christian church? Wherever we see such ugly traits as pride, jealousy, gossip and backbiting, what are we to conclude about those who call themselves Christian yet seem to bear none of the fruit of the Spirit? Is Paul stating an ideal toward which we should strive or is he declaring the basic standard which must be met?

Since sin appears to dog the steps of all believers ("If we claim to be without sin . . . the truth is not in us" 1 John 1:8), how can it be said that anyone is a child of God? Just how much leading of the Spirit does it take to qualify as a son of God? How much resistance to God's leading does it take to disqualify a person from being a son of God?

Are these kinds of questions valid? Are they misleading? Do you think they may be essentially unanswerable? Why? Why not?

8

The Triumph of Believing

Romans 8:18-39

Paul would be the last person in the world to say that once you become a Christian all your problems will be over. On one occasion he listed some of the trials he had to put up with. He spoke among other things of being thrown into prison and flogged, of being exposed to death again and again, of shipwrecks, dangers, and sleepless labor (see 2 Cor. 11:23-29). The walk of faith is no bed of roses. Sharing in the sufferings of Christ (as Paul called it) is a necessary prelude to sharing in His glory.

Yet all such suffering in the present time is not worthy of comparison with the glory that awaits the child of God. And even as he waits he is supported by the intercessory prayers of the Spirit and the knowledge that all things work together for his good. Best of all there is no one or no thing in all creation that could ever separate him from the love of God. This is the message of Romans 8:18-39.

Our Present Suffering

The problems of this life, says Paul, are trivial in comparison with the glory which is about to *burst upon us* (see v. 18); (the note of immediacy is overlooked by translators who neglect the significance of the Greek *mellousan*). The glory of which Paul speaks is the divine radiance which was lost in the Fall and will be restored at the end of the age (see Rom. 3:23).

It is typically human to get so involved in the immediate trials of life that we lose sight of how it will all turn out. We need to be reminded that for the moment we are on a detour marked "suffering," but just around the corner is our destination—eternal joy. The troubles we face for a short time now (after all, how long is a lifetime when compared with eternity?) are not even worth considering when compared with the rapture of God's presence which will continue forever. We need to remember that "what is seen is temporary, but what is unseen is eternal" (2 Cor. 4:18).

The day is almost here when we will discard the rags of our mortality and don the robes of immortality. Darkness will turn to day and we will become in fact what God intended we should be—His glorious creation, children of God reflecting the perfection and love of their heavenly Father.

Not only do we await this day of transformation, but the creation as well "waits in eager expectation for the sons of God to be revealed" (Rom. 8:19). The created universe is personified as frustrated by man's sin and involved in the death and decay which sin brought about. But it too awaits that great day when it will share in the glorious freedom of the children of God (see vv. 19-21).

Creation was subjected to decay and bondage not through some fault of its own but because of the sin of man. Paul undoubtedly alludes to the account in Genesis 3. To Adam, God said, "Because you listened to your wife and ate from the tree . . . cursed is the ground because of you. . . . It will produce thorns and thistles for you" (Gen. 3:17,18). Not only did Adam's sin bring ruin to the human family, it brought the "tyranny of change and decay" (Rom. 8:21, *Phillips*) to nature as well. But now "the whole creation is on tiptoe to see the wonderful sight of the sons of God coming into their own" (v. 19, *Phillips*). The Greek verb is picturesque. Literally it means, "to stretch the head forward." In context it portrays the entire created universe with its head stretched forward looking intently for the first rays of the dawning age—that age when the children of God will be transformed and creation will share in their glorious release from corruption and decay.

It is obvious that the created order has been groaning in a sort of universal travail "right up to the present time" (v. 22). She is undergoing the pains of childbirth but has not as yet delivered. And we (the church), along with her, groan inwardly as we eagerly await the day when our sonship will be complete.

The final stage of our adoption will be "the redemption of our bodies" (v. 23). Unlike nature, however, we have the "firstfruits of the Spirit." The term for "firstfruits" is taken from the legal and commercial life of antiquity. It designated a deposit or down payment which was part of the total price and established a legal claim on the product. It was the earnest money which ratified a contractual agreement. The "firstfruits of the Spirit" would be the presence and work of the Holy Spirit in the life of the believer. His presence, which leads us to cry, "*Abba*, Father" (8:15), is the absolute guarantee that one day our adoption into the family of God will be full and complete. Our status as sons of God is secure. On that glorious day when our bodies are released from the bondage of decay (see 1 Cor. 15:51-54) and we become like Him (see 1 John 3:2) our adoption into His family will be complete.

It is in this hope that our salvation lies. If we already had what we hoped for there would be no further need for hope (see Rom. 8:24). But since we are hoping for that which we do not as yet have, we must continue to wait with patience (see v. 25). Hope is an integral part of the Christian experience. It testifies to the fact that something of importance lies in the future. Hope keeps us from becoming so absorbed in the present that we forget the promises of God regarding the future. It prevents us from so fixing our gaze on what is that we lose sight of what will be. Saving faith trusts God for what He has done; saving hope trusts Him for what He will do.

Helped While We Wait

It is clear that living as a Christian in a world dominated and controlled by sin will inevitably involve suffering. To Timothy Paul writes, "Everyone who wants to live a godly life in Christ Jesus will be persecuted" (2 Tim. 3:12). We are not left alone in our trials however. In the five verses under consideration in Romans 8:26-30 Paul tells us of two major sources of help. First, the intercessory prayers of the Holy Spirit, and secondly, the knowledge that all things work together for the good of those who love God.

"In the same way" (that is, just as "the whole creation has been groaning" v. 22, and we ourselves "groan inwardly" v. 23) the Spirit helps us in our weakness by interceding for us "with groans that words cannot express" (v. 26). Some have suggested that this last phrase means *unspoken* rather than inexpressible groans. Cranfield argues from the following verse that since God already knows the Spirit's intention it would not have to be expressed in words. The phrase is more correctly understood as indicating the spiritual depth and intensity of the actual prayer. From time to time we find ourselves at a loss to put into words the deepest desires of our heart. This same intensity is true of the prayers of the Spirit. He great fervor.

The *NIV* says that "we do not know how we ought to
pray." *Lamsa* is right when he translates, "what is right
and proper for us to pray for." It is not a question of *how*
we are to pray, as if God is concerned with our method of
praying. Prayer is designed for the helpless and the helpless cannot be asked to measure up to some arbitrary
standard of acceptability. It is rather a question of *what* we
should pray for. In times of distress it is difficult to know
whether we should ask for a change of circumstance or for
the strength to endure. This comes from our human frailty, our "weakness" Paul calls it. Because we do not know
what to pray for, the Spirit takes over the task and intercedes on our behalf to God.

The intercessory work of Jesus, the great high priest
of the order of Melchizedek, is well known to most
Christians. "He is able to save completely those who
come to God through him, because he always lives to
intercede for them" (Heb. 7:25). Our sins merit God's
wrath but Jesus stands at the right hand of God con-
tinuously presenting the evidence that the punishment we
deserve has already been paid by His own death on the
cross. He is our intercessor. We sometimes forget,
however, that the Holy Spirit also pleads our case. In our
perplexity concerning what we ought to pray for, the
Spirit joins us in prayer and intercedes on our behalf with
sighs too deep for words. He "helps us in our weakness"
(Rom. 8:26).

In passing it should be noted that some writers take
this groaning to be *our* groaning and interpret the verse as
speaking in tongues. That may be the understanding of the
NEB which says, "Through our inarticulate groans the
Spirit himself is pleading for us." The groaning, however,

is that of the Spirit and is linked with our groans and those of creation.

The great value of the Spirit's intercession is that God who knows the heart is certainly able to understand what it is that His Spirit is requesting. God is able to answer the Spirit's prayers "because his [the Spirit's] intercessions for the saints are in harmony with God's will" (v. 27, *Weymouth*). We are strengthened in our suffering by realizing that not only does the Spirit pray for us but God understands His prayers completely and can answer them because they are always in accordance with His will.

"Prayer," writes Frank Laubach, is "the mightiest force in the world." It is God acting in response to our requests. When we ask according to His will He delights to answer. Part of our problem is that our understanding of what God truly desires is less than perfect. Our understanding is limited by our finiteness and clouded by the lingering influence of our fallen nature. Not so, the Holy Spirit. God's Spirit is God and He understands with perfect clarity the divine intention. His prayers are *always* answered. And He it is who intercedes for us with inexpressible yearning. In our weakness we are not alone. In our perplexity about what we should pray for, the Spirit steps in and takes over the responsibility of interpreting to God what He knows will be best. Small wonder that Jesus calls Him a Paraclete, one "called alongside" to help.

We come now to a second source of help as we await the coming glory. It is the realization that all things, even the trials that we must suffer, work together for our good (vv. 28-30). Romans 8:28 has long been a great source of spiritual comfort and encouragement to believers undergoing severe trial. Let us look at it closely.

You may have noticed from reading several modern speech translations that there are two basic ways of interpreting verse 28. Either *God* works in all things (or causes all things to work together) for the good of those who love him, or *all things* work together to that end. The first option requires the addition of the word "God" to the Greek text (supported by some manuscripts but not the preferred reading). The second must answer the argument that "all things working together for good" is a sort of "evolutionary optimism" that runs counter to what we know of Paul. The idea that whatever happens to a good man ultimately turns out for his benefit is widespread in ancient literature. One rabbi said that "for the godly man all things, even though for others they are evils, are beneficial." Plato, addressing the gentlemen of the jury, said they must be convinced of one basic truth, "that no evil befalls a good man either in life or after death."

Paul's conviction, however, is not based upon the questionable assumption that everything has a way of turning out okay. He is not concurring with a broad secular hope that goodness will somehow prevail over evil. His "optimism" is limited to "those who keep on loving God" (*Williams*). Whatever the relationship of Paul's phraseology to that of the religious and secular world of his day, the important fact is that for Paul the truth is grounded in God's revelation of Himself in Christ Jesus. This alone radically transforms the popular idea. It is for those alone who by faith accept this revelation that everything works together for good.

Lest loving God appear to be a meritorious act, Paul proceeds immediately to define those who love God as those "who have been called according to his purpose." Our love is a response to His call, and His call is the historical expression of His eternal purpose.

It is important that the believer take "all things" in the fullest possible sense. (I prefer the "shorter reading" which makes "all things" the subject of "work together"—"We know that all things work together"—over the longer reading which adds "God" for that purpose.) Paul does not say "almost everything." It is difficult to understand how sin and sorrow could possibly qualify as working for our good. In an otherwise perfect world they wouldn't. But we live in a fallen world and find ourselves, more often than we would wish, caught up in some failing which in itself must be understood as damaging. And in itself it is. But it is one of the "all things" which, if we love God, will work for our good. Of course, we must *let* it work for our good. We cannot continue on the false premise that more of the same will work for our greater good. To follow such a course would be to demonstrate that we in fact do not love God.

Sorrow is a normal part of the world in which we live. Setbacks are common. Things don't always work out as we have planned. Disasters happen. We are all under the condemnation of physical death. Yet all of these can and *do* work for the good (not necessarily for the convenience or the immediate pleasure) of those who are called according to the will of God. An old poem says:

> I walked a mile with Pleasure,
>   She chattered all the way:
> But I was none the wiser
>   For all she had to say.
> Then I walked a mile with Sorrow,
>   And ne'er a word said she;
> But Oh the lessons I did learn,
>   When Sorrow walked with me.

Verses 29-30 present a five-step development that reaches from eternity past to eternity future. The verses do not, however, give us a rigid and deterministic theology. Barclay calls it a "lyrical expression of Christian experience."

The sequence begins with foreknowledge: "For those God foreknew he also predestined" (v. 29). This does not teach that God predestined man on the basis of what He knew ahead of time that man would do. Theologians tell us that God can only know (in a biblical sense) what He has already determined should be. At the origin of it all are the will and pleasure of a sovereign God. God's foreknowledge is one with His foreordination, not some sort of prior step. Both have existed from before the foundation of the world (see Eph. 1:4; 2 Tim. 1:9).

Notice that predestination, in this context, is not to salvation but to being conformed to the likeness of Christ. God had an ethical and moral goal in mind. He determined from the beginning that those whom He would redeem should be "moulded into the image of his Son" (*Knox*). As a first step they would need to come to Christ. But the purpose of a predestination goes far beyond that initial step. In becoming "conformed to the likeness of [God's] Son" they would become the "many brothers" of Christ (v. 29); Christ the firstborn, we His brothers. This is what God purposed. His desire is that Christ might be the eldest in a vast family of brothers, all of whom share a family likeness.

Predestination leads to calling. Now we enter historical time. God calls us "out of darkness into his wonderful light" (1 Pet. 2:9), "into fellowship with his Son" (1 Cor. 1:9), and "to his eternal glory in Christ" (1 Pet. 5:10). God's call is an effectual call, that is, it achieves its purpose. Those whom God called "he also justified" (Rom. 8:30). His calling resulted in our being declared righteous. Those whom He brought into a right-standing with Himself He also glorified. Note that "glorified" is in the past tense. In a sense we have been given a foretaste of the glory which shall be ours. It is better, however, to keep the focus on our future glorification—that time yet to come when we shall pass from this earthly existence marked by sin to enter the eternal realm of God's glorious presence. The verb is past tense because the event is so certain. Like the prophets who regularly spoke of future events as having taken place, Paul is so certain that God will glorify those He has chosen that he can declare it to already be a fact. Personal confidence in God's sovereign ways along with the intercessory prayers of the Spirit strengthens believers during their time of waiting.

Secure Forever

We come now to the conclusion not only to the question of Christian suffering—Romans 8:18—but also to the entire epistle up to this point. God has provided by the death of His Son a righteousness for all who believe (see 3:21-26). He showers us with the benefits of believing (see 5:1-11) and provides us His Spirit for victory over sin (see 8:1-17). "What, then, shall we say in response to this? If God is for us, who can be against us?" (8:31).

Obviously, these are rhetorical questions. They are asked for effect and expect no answer. *Phillips* translates the first, "In face of all this, what is there left to say?" God's provision for His children leaves us speechless! With God on our side it couldn't matter less who might be against us. Like a small boy in the company of an older brother we walk through life unconcerned about opposition that would terrify us if we were alone. God for us is the heart of the good news. He took the initiative and came to our aid. Even when as sinners we rejected His love, "Christ died for us" (Rom. 5:8). Since God loves us,

Christ died for us, and the Spirit "intercedes for us" (8:26), it can rightly be said that the entire trinity— Father, Son, and Holy Spirit—is entirely on our side. No wonder Paul writes, "What is there left to say!" (*Phillips*)

Verse 32 indicates exactly *how* God is for us. First of all, He is for us in that He "did not spare his own Son, but gave him up for us all." Paul uses the words that God spoke to Abraham on the occasion of the sacrifice of Isaac—"Now I know that you fear God, because *you have not withheld from me your son, your only son*" (Gen. 22:12, italics added). As Abraham was willing to give his son in loyal obedience to divine command so also does God sacrifice His Son on our behalf.

But God is also for us in that along with the gift of His Son He "graciously gives us all things" (8:32). God lavishes upon us (the emphasis of the word in Greek is on the sheer goodness of the gift) all that He has to give. In Christ we fall heir to every spiritual blessing. We are the most highly favored of all mankind.

Verses 33, 34 are punctuated in several different ways resulting in slightly different interpretations. I find the approach of the *NIV* quite convincing (although other punctuations yield similar conclusions). The verses contain two parallel rhetorical questions followed by two responses.

Question one: "Who will bring any charge against those whom God has chosen?" (v. 33). This essentially repeats the earlier question in verse 31b. Who could ever successfully lodge a complaint against someone chosen by God? God is the One who has already pronounced the believer righteous. Will the judge who has reached his verdict on the clear evidence that the penalty has been paid now reverse himself and exact further payment? Never!

Question two: "Who is he that condemns?" (v. 34). With the penalty for sin paid in full, who is left to make accusation? It certainly isn't Christ Jesus because He is the one who died for us. Not only that, but He was raised to life and is now at the place of highest honor pleading our case to God (see v. 34). Whatever false accusation that might be raised against us is immediately countered by the ceaseless intercession of the Lamb of God—the very One whose death provided the basis of our salvation.

But is it somehow possible that we could be separated from God and all that He has accomplished on our behalf? Knowing that no answer could ever be forthcoming, Paul triumphantly asks, "Who shall separate us from the love of Christ?" (v. 35). Can anything drive a wedge between the Christian and his Lord? "Shall trouble or hardship or persecution or famine or nakedness or danger or sword?" (v. 35). These are among the present sufferings (see v. 18) that accompany the life of the Christian in this world. But could they ever separate the believer from the love which Christ has for His own?

A quotation from Psalm 44:22 is added to remind the church that the people of God have always faced tribulation and extreme privation: "For your sake we face death all day long; we are considered as sheep to be slaughtered" (Rom. 8:36).

Now for the answer. "No, in all these things we are more than conquerors through him who loved us" (v. 37). Because we have experienced the transforming power of the love of God not only can we conquer the problems and setbacks of life but we can "over-conquer," that is we can take the obstacle and use it as a stepping stone. That which was meant for our defeat becomes the instrument of our victory. This is what it means to *more than conquer*.

Paul's final words cannot be improved by comment.

They are the finest expression of religious exaltation ever recorded. Read them slowly and let God's Spirit bring home their full spiritual impact. "For I am convinced that neither death nor life, neither angels nor demons, neither the present nor the future, nor any powers, neither height nor depth, nor anything else in all creation, will be able to separate us from the love of God that is in Christ Jesus our Lord" (vv. 38, 39).

For Discussion

Love is an active power. It is the only force that can ever conquer its opposition. To return hate for hate is to increase the hatred. To counter aggression with force is to intensify the conflict. Only love can change its opposition. Hate and bitterness can reach a standoff but only love can effect a reconciliation.

Have you ever viewed love as an active force in interpersonal relations? Have you ever tried combating antagonism with love? Do you find it difficult to dislike a person who obviously thinks a great deal of you?

Would you be willing to try an experiment? Single out one person with whom you are not friends. Go out of your way to place the welfare of that person above your own (remember, love is not an emotion; it is a decision of the will). Do you think you will possibly be able to go on disliking this person? What will be his/her response to your love? Is love an active power? God loves you; will you extend that courtesy to others?

9

What About the Jews?

Romans 3:1-4; 9:1—11:32

If circumcision is without value to the Jew who breaks the law (see Rom. 2:25) and if "a man is not a Jew if he is only one outwardly" (2:28), then it must be asked, "What advantage, then, is there in being a Jew, or what value is there in circumcision?" (3:1). Apparently there is no advantage in being a Jew nor is circumcision of any value. Paul doesn't fall into the trap of unnecessarily offending Jewish national sentiment; besides, it's also bad theology. The entire Old Testament bears witness to the fact that the Jewish people had received God's special favor. Their role as the people of God was intended to issue in responsible action rather than personal enjoyment. The fundamental problem of the Jew was that he misunderstood the implications of being chosen by God.

So instead of playing down the advantages of being a Jew, Paul responds to the question with a resounding, "Much in every way!" Then he starts listing the advantages. "First of all they have been entrusted with the very words of God" (v. 2). The oracles (or *logia*) of God are the utterances of God. Paul referred, of course, to the Old Testament. The Jewish people were privileged to have been the nation to whom God had delivered His messages. They were the scribes who recorded and preserved what God had said and done in sacred history. Even if some of them had been unfaithful God would never break His covenant with Israel (see vv. 3,4). God remains true even though this would make every man a liar. God does not rescind the favor which He has extended throughout history to His own people, the Jews.

At this point Paul is detracted from his line of argument. He sets aside the question of how the gospel affects God's relationship to His Old Testament people while he takes care of several other important points that belong to his argument. In fact, Paul doesn't return to the question of the Jew until chapter 9. There, and in the two following chapters, he discusses the issue at considerable length. Our approach to this section will be to follow Paul's basic line of argument and comment on several points of special interest.

It Was Israel, Not God, That Failed

It is important to remember that the basic theme of Romans 9-11 is not the future of the Jewish race but the character of God. Why has God, who first elected the Jews, now turned His attention to the Gentiles? What are we to understand in respect to His age-long involvement with the people of Israel? Has that special relationship come to an end in that salvation is now extended to all who will accept it by faith? Has God acted in a capricious and arbitrary fashion? If so, what kind of a God is He?

The first subsection is 9:1-5. In it the apostle laments over his kinsmen by race. Paul could never forget the fact that he was a Jew. Although he had been commissioned an apostle to the Gentiles (see Gal. 2:8) he carried in his heart an unceasing anguish for his Jewish brethren. So profound was his sorrow for their spiritual condition that he would willingly be cut off from Christ if it would restore them to their intended position (Rom 9:3). Their blessings have been great beyond comparison. To them belonged the rights of sonship, the glory of the divine presence, and the covenants between God and man. Futhermore, they received instruction in the law, a guide to worship in the Temple, and the promise of a divinely ordered destiny. They themselves are direct descendants of the patriarchs. One of their number (as far as his human ancestry is concerned) was none other than Christ, the Messiah. "Blessed forevermore be the God who is over all! Amen" (9:5, *Moffatt*) is the only appropriate response of the spiritually sensitive heart.

Verses 6-13 establish the point that Israel's failure is her own. Her rejection of Christ does not mean that God has failed to keep His promise. He has not severed ties with the true Israel. It should be clear that not everyone who is descended from Israel is a true Israelite (see v. 6). Not every Israelite is a child of Abraham. Biblical history demonstrates that God's selective process has involved exclusion as well as inclusion. Ishmael was the son of Abraham and Hagar, the Egyptian maidservant. Although he became the head of a great nation he and his descendants were never counted among the people of God. Abraham's line of descent ran through Isaac, the son of promise (see v. 8). Although both Ishmael and Isaac were equally the natural children of Abraham, only the descendants of Isaac are children of the promise and consequently Abraham's offspring.

The same is true of Jacob and Esau, twin brothers born to Isaac and Rebecca. Even before they were born— before either one had done anything good or bad—God chose Jacob saying, "Jacob I loved, but Esau I hated" (9:13; a Hebrew idiom indicating preference for one over the other). God's selection rests not on what a person has done but upon His own sovereign will. Thus the fact that

Israel has failed does not mean that God has broken His promise. His promise was made to the "Israel within Israel." To trace one's human lineage does not make one a child of promise. Historically God has chosen on the basis of His own free will.

But the question arises, Doesn't such a highly arbitrary procedure imply injustice on God's part? The first of two basic questions posed in verses 14-29 is, "What then shall we say? Is God unjust?" (v. 14). The immediate response is, "Not at all!" Paul then cites God's words to Moses, "I will have mercy on whom I have mercy, and I will have compassion on whom I have compassion" (v. 15). Commentators stress the importance of this verse for a proper understanding of the entire section. God's elective process is not an exercise of unqualified freedom. It reflects, rather, the freedom of His mercy. Whatever God does for man He does out of mercy and compassion. Since God owes no man anything, His selection of some does not make Him unjust to others. God's sovereignty is also seen in His raising up of Pharaoh, that "dark prototype of all the rejected in Israel" (*Barth*). As Pharaoh's plans were overruled in accordance with God's purpose, so also will the plans of the disobedient Israel be brought to nothing. Both the showing of mercy and the hardening of the heart are expressions of the divine will operating out of compassion for man.

A second question arises immediately—If God does what He wants, "Then why does [he] still blame us? For who resists his will?" (v. 19). If man is a pawn in God's hand how can God blame him for what happens? Is it not morally wrong to assign responsibility for something over which a person has no control?

Paul's answer is straightforward and blunt—"Who are you, O man, to talk back to God?" (v. 20). Can the pot say to the potter, "Why did you make me like this?" Doesn't the potter have the right to do what he wants to with the clay? Can't he take one lump of clay and make from it vessels—some for a noble and others for a menial purpose? Some writers have reacted strongly against Paul's argument. Dodd says that the analogy of man as a pot "is the weakest point in the whole epistle."

But what is the central point of the analogy? Is it not that God, rather than man, is responsible for the outcome of history (as the potter, not the pot, is responsible for what he produces)? In calling both Jew and Gentile into fellowship with Himself it is God who bears the responsibility for the final outcome. Man has no cause to quibble. He forfeited everything by his sin and it is only by the mercy of God that any are selected for divine favor. The inclusion of the Gentiles was foretold in prophetic Scripture. Hosea says that those who are not God's people will be called "sons of the living God" (v. 26). And Isaiah prophesied that although the Israelites should be in number "like the sand by the sea, only the remnant will be saved" (v. 27). Thus the Old Testament itself teaches that only some of the Jews will be saved and that Gentiles will become a part of the people of God.

How Israel Came to Fail

What, then, is the conclusion? Is it not that the Gentiles, who did not have the Law's standard of righteousness as a guide, nevertheless obtained righteousness, but Israel, who pursued a righteousness based on Law, did not succeed in fulfilling that Law? Gentiles living outside the Law received righteousness while Israel trying to keep the Law failed.

And why did Israel fail? Because their efforts were based on works not on faith. The operating principle which leads to a right-standing before God is faith in what He has done, not confidence in our own ability to gain God's favor by meritorious actions. The gospel is God's proclamation that He has done all that is required. Man's responsibility is to accept it by faith. Israel stumbled over this obstacle. Her determination to establish her own righteousness made her blind to the righteousness which Christ offered as a free gift.

Chapter 10 clarifies and enlarges upon the theme of Israel's disobedience. Verses 1-13 contrast righteousness based on law and righteousness which results from faith. Verses 14-21 demonstrate that Israel is without excuse for her failure.

Paul has a deep concern for the salvation of his Jewish brethren. He knows from his own involvement in Judaism that they are zealous for God. Unfortunately their zeal is not guided by true insight. Disregarding God's way to receive righteousness they plunged ahead in a vain attempt to establish their own. They did not realize that "Christ is the end of the law" (10:4). He is the end of the Law not only in a temporal sense (the struggle for righteousness by Law is over) but also in the sense of its goal (He fulfills in Himself the intention of the Law). Since He is the end of the Law there is now "righteousness for everyone who believes" (v. 4). In that the demands of the Law have been perfectly met in Him, righteousness is no longer a matter of human striving but of divine favor.

Moses had something to say about law-righteousness: "Anyone who can perform it, shall live by it" (v. 5, *Moffatt*). The obvious problem is that no one can carry out its demands. On the other hand, the righteousness based on faith says that it is unnecessary to scale heaven and bring Christ down or descend into the abyss to bring Him back from the dead because the message about faith is already within reach (see vv. 5-8). And what is that message? Simply this: "If you openly confess that Jesus is Lord and believe in your heart that God raised him from the dead, then you will be saved" (see v. 9). When a person believes, he is justified, and in confessing this belief his salvation is confirmed.

The confession "Jesus is Lord" is the earliest creed of the Christian church. Some think that it arose during times of persecution in response to the empire's insistence that her citizens acknowledge "Caesar is Lord." Its roots go deeper, however. The Greek word *kurios* served both as an expression of respect ("sir") and as a normal title for emperors and gods. More importantly for the early church is the fact that *kurios* occurs more than 6,000 times in the Greek Old Testament as the name of God. Peter concludes his Pentecost sermon with the declaration that "God has made this Jesus, whom you crucified, both Lord [*kurios*] and Christ" (Acts 2:36). Cranfield writes, "The confession that Jesus is Lord meant the acknowledgment that Jesus shares the name and the nature, the holiness, the authority, power, majesty and eternity of the one and only true God." It takes faith to acknowledge Jesus as Lord! And the open confession of this faith brings salvation.

Because righteousness comes by faith it matters not whether the believer is Jew or Gentile. The same Lord blesses all who call on Him and "everyone who calls on the name of the Lord will be saved" (Rom. 10:13).

Now come the excuses. You say that salvation results from calling "on the name of the Lord" (v. 13) but how can anyone call on One in whom they haven't believed? And doesn't believing depend on hearing, and hearing on someone preaching? Furthermore, "How can they preach unless they are sent?" (v. 15). In short, isn't Israel's failure due to never having had a chance to hear?

Oh no, says Paul. Isaiah described the messengers who came bearing "glad tidings of good things" (v. 15, *KJV*; see also Isa. 52:7). You cannot claim that you never heard the message; you all heard it but not everyone responded. As Isaiah said, "Lord, who has believed our message?" (v. 16; see also Isa. 53:1). Of course the Israelites heard the message. As Psalm 19 declares, It has gone all over the earth and reached men everywhere (see Rom. 10:18; see also Ps. 19:4).

But what if Israel didn't understand? Perhaps the message was so difficult that Israel was unable to grasp its significance. Hardly, retorts Paul. Let me cite as a primary reference your own lawgiver, Moses. He spoke of a nation void of understanding that would arouse your envy and anger (see Rom 10:19). If that nation (which is no nation in God's sight) understood the concept of righteousness by faith, how can you possibly argue that it is too difficult? Isaiah put it even more boldly. He has God saying, "I was found by those [not seeking] me; I revealed myself to those who [hadn't asked]" (v. 20). If these Gentiles grasped the message there is no excuse for the Jews. The real problem is that you are, as Isaiah also said, "a disobedient and obstinate people" (v. 21; see also Isa. 65:2). You missed the way of righteousness by faith, not because you never heard of it nor because you couldn't understand it, but because you adamantly refused to accept it. You are "a self-willed and fault-finding people" (*Weymouth*).

God's Plan for the Jew

If the conclusion thus far is that Israel is a willful and disobedient people, determined to pursue righteousness by a method bound to fail, then does it not follow that for all practical purposes God has rejected His people (see

11:1)? "By no means!" answers Paul. "I myself am an Israelite and God has not rejected me." Historically there has always been a believing remnant. Remember when Elijah complained to God about how all the prophets had been killed and he alone was left (and his enemies were trying to kill him?)! God said, "There are 7,000 who haven't bowed the knee to Baal" (see 11:4). God has always preserved a remnant. As of old, so also at the present time there remains "a remnant chosen by grace" (v. 5). God has taken the initiative in preserving for Himself a portion of Israel. If a person were able to earn a place in this remnant then the privilege would no longer be based on the principle of unmerited favor.

So this is the situation. Israel as a nation, in spite of their earnest seeking, did not find what they were looking for—a right-standing before God. But the chosen remnant did (see v. 7). And what about the others? They became "hardened" (the word is a medical term and means to form a callous). To reject the truth is spiritual suicide. Disobedience makes a person insensitive to the appeal of God. As the Old Testament says, "God has numbed their senses" (v. 8, *Knox*), "he gave them blind eyes and deaf ears, and so it is still" (*NEB*). David, as well, spoke of their "bondage and blindness" (v. 10).

There is no question but that the Jews have stumbled. The crucial issue is, however, are they permanently out of the race? Are they "beyond recovery" (v. 11)? "Not at all!" answers Paul. And now we come to the unfolding of God's plan for the Jews. Because of their disobedience salvation has come to the Gentiles. But watch what happens. This in turn will rouse the envy of the Jews. Just think—if the transgression of the Jews has enriched the Gentiles, how much greater will be the blessing of their full restoration (see v. 12).

This fundamental insight is repeated and enlarged in the paragraph which follows (vv. 13-16). Paul takes pride in his ministry to the Gentiles, hoping that in this way he can stir his countrymen to envy and bring some to salvation. If their rejection brought reconciliation to the world, then their acceptance must be considered a resurrection from the dead (see v. 15). Take hope. "If the root is holy, so are the branches" (v. 16); that is, since Abraham and the patriarchs were consecrated to God, so also is the whole nation set apart in a special way.

Reference to the root and branches leads Paul to expand his theme with a related metaphor (vv. 17-24). Consider an olive tree whose natural branches have been broken off so that wild olive shoots might be grafted in. The domestic olive tree is Israel. Its natural branches (Jewish people) were broken off "because of unbelief" (v. 20). You Gentiles (see v. 13) are the wild olive shoots that have been grafted in and draw nourishment from the root (see v. 17). Do not be arrogant about the branches that have been cut off. Remember that it is the root that supports you (see v. 18) and that if God did not spare the natural branches neither will He spare you (if you follow their course of action).

Consider both "the kindness and sternness of God" (v. 22)—how He dealt in strict justice to those who disobeyed, but in kindness to you. He will continue in the same way; of course, provided you remain responsive to that kindness. If not, you will be cut off as well. But note that if the Jews do not continue in their unbelief God will graft them back into the tree (see v. 23). After all, it's easier to graft a natural branch than a wild one (see v. 24)!

We arrive now at the conclusion of Paul's lengthy discussion on God's plan for the Jew. He calls it a "mystery" (v. 25), that is, a truth which can be known only by revelation, once hidden but now disclosed to all who will hear. Paul shares the mystery with the believing Gentiles so that they will remain humble and not think too highly of themselves. The mystery has been hinted at in preceding verses—12, 15, 23, 24—now it is clearly stated. It involves three stages in the fulfillment of the divine plan for salvation.

The first part of God's plan is the hardening of a part of Israel (not a partial hardening). That took place when the nation rejected God's way to attain righteousness. Secondly, this hardening will continue until the full complement of Gentiles has come in. Finally, "And so all Israel will be saved" (v. 26). This is the crucial statement. Of the many interpretations which have been suggested I find the following to be the most satisfactory. "And so" is an emphatic way of saying "in this way, and only in this way." "All Israel" refers to the nation Israel as a whole but not necessarily to every individual.

Thus Paul is saying, God's plan for the salvation of man involves three stages: (1) the believing remnant, (2) the Gentiles, (3) Israel as a whole. Most of the standard commentaries on Romans hold that Paul is here teaching the salvation of Israel as an eschatological event. Note that Paul says nothing about the reestablishment of a national state. For Israel to be saved she will have to come by the way of faith. Paul saw God's favor to the Gentiles as prompting this movement of national repentance. He turns immediately to Scripture for confirmation: "The deliverer will come from Zion; he will turn godlessness away from Jacob" (v. 26). "They shall see the fulfilment of my Covenant when I take away their sins" (v. 27, *TCNT*).

Israel may be temporarily rejected by God for the benefit of the Gentiles, but from the standpoint of God's elective purpose the Jewish people are loved by Him "on account of the patriarchs" (v. 28). Remember, the gifts and call of God "are irrevocable" (v. 29)! You Gentiles were disobedient but now enjoy God's mercy "in the day of their disobedience" (*TCNT*). They have "now become disobedient in order that they too may now receive mercy" (v. 31). What this amounts to is that "God has bound all men over to disobedience so that he may have mercy on them all" (v. 32). As Barrett puts it, "Every man must be damned if he is to be justified."

Paul's argument is now complete. God did elect Israel and consequently blessed her in many ways. Her insistence upon seeking righteousness by works led to a rejection of all but the remnant. In turning to the Gentiles He not only fulfilled Old Testament promise but also provided the motivation for Israel's return. In the end she will respond in faith and "all Israel will be saved" (v. 26). The apostle closes the chapter, verses 33-36, with a rhapsody of praise. He confesses the depths of the wisdom of God and the inscrutable nature of His actions. God is beyond human ken. No one has known His mind or given Him advice. In Him all things find their origin, their impulse and the center of their being. "To him be the glory for ever! Amen" (v. 36).

For Discussion

There are biblical scholars who understand Romans 11:26 in a different way. They see in this passage warrant for the establishment of the modern state of Israel. The year 1948 becomes a pivotal date in the fulfillment of prophecy. Some teach that the Temple will be rebuilt in Jerusalem and that animal sacrifices will be reinstated.

Obviously this view goes beyond the verse in question. But does the line of thought in chapters 9-11 favor the interpretation? Would not reverting to a form of Old Testament sacrificial practice move away from the principle of faith and back toward a righteousness by works? How does 10:4 with its insistence that "Christ is the end of the law" relate to this question? Do you recall why Paul shared this understanding of the future of the Jew (see 11:25)?

Practical Christianity

Romans 12:1-2,9-13

With chapter 12 we begin the last major division of the book of Romans (12:1—15:13). As in a number of his other letters Paul now shifts his attention from the broader sweep of theology to the more specific and practical concerns of daily living. The first two verses of chapter 12 serve as an appropriate bridge in that they state with clarity the essential connection between doctrine and ethics. The specific injunctions which follow grow out of and give expression to the ethical perspective established in the opening verses. In our discussion we will first study with care the basis for Christian ethics (12:1,2) and then turn to "twelve telegraphic rules" for everyday Christian living (12:9-13).

As we move into this section it is important to note that we are not deserting "salvation by faith alone" and falling back into legalism. The obedience expected is not intended as a way to gain God's favor. It is what Paul in 16:26 will call the "obedience inspired by faith" (*Williams*). Peter makes the same point when he speaks of the elect as chosen "for obedience to Jesus Christ" (1 Pet. 1:2). The obedience of the believer is an expression of his gratitude to God. It is not what he *must* do (in order to be justified) but what he is unable not to do (because he is justified). Obedience of this sort is a necessary expression of spiritual transformation. It is personal, spontaneous and joyful—the natural response of a heart genuinely touched by the love of God.

The Transformed Life

Our new section begins with the important word, "therefore." As a transition word it ties together all that follows with everything that has come before. In context it indicates that the basis for all moral effort on the part of the Christian lies in the saving activity of God. "Therefore," writes Paul, "I urge you, brothers, in view of God's mercy, to offer [yourselves] as living sacrifices." And what are the mercies (the Greek is plural) of God which Paul has mentioned? Supremely the redemptive sacrifice of His Son (see 3:25), but also righteousness by faith (see 3:22), "peace with God" (5:1), reconciliation (see 5:10,11), freedom from the power of sin (see 6:18), the abiding presence of His Spirit (see 8:11), adoption into His family (see 8:15,16), a love from which we can never be separated (see 8:38,39), and the firm assurance that He never goes back on His word (chapters 9-11).

On the basis of these acts of divine compassion Paul now urges the believers at Rome to offer themselves as a sacrifice to God. The word translated "urge" (in the *NIV*) was a technical term for Christian exhortation. The apostle is not begging his readers to do God a favor. The charge is delivered as an authoritative summons to obedience based on the truth of the gospel. To view God as a helpless giant pleading with disobedient dwarfs demeans His character. His exhortation to obedience is a subpoena, not a hopeful request; we disregard it at our own risk!

The language of verse 1 is sacrificial. To offer oneself translates a verb which in extra-biblical Greek was used for ritual sacrifice. The tense of the imperative (aorist) has led some translators to reflect in their rendering the idea of a definite once-for-all self-surrender. *Williams* has, "Make a decisive dedication of your bodies." Bodies, of course, refers not to one's physical being (in contrast to psychic or spiritual existence) but to all that we are in our relation to the demands of life. In another place Paul directs us in similar fashion to "honor God with [our] body" (1 Cor. 6:20). The point is that our dedication to God should not rest in the lofty realm of theory and ideal, but be carried out on the practical plane of what we actually do through the bodies in which we live.

So we are to present ourselves as a sacrifice to God. Most translators join the first of the three qualifying adjectives (living, holy, acceptable) directly to the noun. We are to be "living sacrifices" (in contrast to the dead sacrifices of ancient ritual). While this makes a good point it is probably not what Paul had in mind. The three descriptive adjectives are parallel and each modifies "sacrifice" in the same way. "Living" means characterized by newness of life (see 6:4); "holy" indicates that we belong entirely to God—we are His property; and "pleasing to God" indicates that we are a true and proper sacrifice, one that He will accept. We belong to God because He created us. We also belong to Him by virtue of our redemption. The final and logical step is to give ourselves voluntarily in free surrender to Him. This sacrifice will be living, holy, and acceptable to God.

A great deal has been written about the final phrase of verse 1—"which is your spiritual worship." The *KJV* has "reasonable service." How can translations differ so radically?

Taking the last term first (worship/service) it is intriguing to trace the history of the Greek word. Originally it meant to work for a wage. Then it came to mean service in a general sense. In certain cases it was used in the context of that for which a man surrenders his life. This led to its distinctive sense of service to God or worship. Thus to worship means to serve. Worship is not something that takes place inside the gothic structure of a sanctuary as much as it is what we do in God's larger "temple," the world in need of the love of Christ expressed through acts of compassion. It's in the shop, the market and the school that we worship (read "serve") God.

The other word, translated "spiritual" in the *NIV*, or "reasonable" in many translations, occurs but twice in the New Testament (1 Pet. 2:2 is the other location). Yet it was a favorite expression of the Greek philosophers. Etymologically it means "rational" or "belonging to the sphere of reason." The Stoics saw it as that which related man to the gods. Thus it came to have the sense of spiritual.

Perhaps the best English translation of the two words is that of *Knox*: "the worship due from you as rational creatures"—however, even here we must keep in mind that, for Paul, *rational* worship/service was not to be defined in terms of its correspondence with the natural rationality of man but with the revelation of God in Christ Jesus. God determines the pattern of rationality. In any case, offering ourselves completely to God is the sacrifice which fulfills our reasonable and spiritual obligations to love and serve the Creator.

Verse 2 tells us to stop doing one thing and allow something else to take place. Paul writes, "Do not conform any longer to the pattern of this world." The significance of the present tenses in the prohibition (Greek) is that something is now going on that should be stopped. We are to stop letting "the world around" us "squeeze" us "into its mold" (*Phillips*). The tendency to allow the prevailing customs and fashions of the world to determine how we organize our lives and set our priorities is greater than we imagine (read Harry Blamires, *The Christian Mind*). Or as a cartoon character said, "The only pressure I can't resist is peer." We have been rescued from this "present evil age" (Gal. 1:4). We should, therefore, stop conforming to its pattern for life.

Rather than conforming to the world we should allow ourselves to be "transformed by the renewing of [our] minds" (Rom. 12:2). In the previous chapters Paul laid out a completely new understanding of life. Justified by faith alone we are freed to allow God's Spirit to energize and control our entire existence. The transformation which God expects is not something that we accomplish through strenuous religious activity. Like everything else, it is a gift. It is important to know that the Greek imperative is passive. *Phillips* has, "Let God remold your minds from within." Some writers emphasize a contrast between the words "conformed" and "transformed" (the first having to do with outward appearance and the second with inner substance) but it is doubtful whether Paul intended such a subtle distinction.

We come now to the purpose for all that has been said thus far. We are to offer ourselves to God, to stop conforming to the customs of society and allow God to change us from within, "in order that we may prove by testing what is the good, pleasing and perfect will of God" (paraphrase). What we have here is essentially a challenge. If we will make a wholehearted surrender to God we will discover that what God has willed for us is good (of intrinsic value and moral worth), pleasing (acceptable to God, meeting all His requirements), and perfect (having completely attained its appropriate end). God's will for us is not designed for our discomfort. It is good, pleasing and perfect. The mean-dispositioned deity who inhabits the heavens of much ill-informed popular thought is not the God of love revealed by Christ Jesus. David complained regarding his enemies, "All day long they twist my words" (Ps. 56:5). God's enemies are still at work twisting men's understanding of the gracious character and loving nature of their heavenly Father.

Twelve Rules to Live By

It is with considerable reluctance that we pass over verses 3-8 of chapter 12. Better to leave them for another book than to do them an injustice by hurrying through. In the space remaining we will look at the 12 concise admonitions found in verses 9-13. Technical scholars demonstrate that this material goes back to a primitive Semitic source. It provides an interesting insight into the life of the very early church. By calling them "rules" we do not mean to imply that they are to be understood legalistically. Codes of conduct need not be considered as limitations on life. They can be regarded as gracious indications of those things which bring pleasure to God and when followed bring the greatest amount of satisfaction to man. God's "rules" are for man's greatest good.

1. "Love must be sincere" (v. 9). Up to this point the noun "love" has been used only of God's love for man (see 5:5,8; 8:35). Now it describes the relationship which the believer owes to his fellowman (see 13:8-10). The Greek word is *agapē*. In the context of biblical revelation it is best defined as the voluntary giving of oneself for the welfare of others. Its unique symbol is the cross.

Our love for others is to be sincere, or genuine. The adjective means "free from hypocrisy or pretense." In fact, the Greek word "sincere" is the word "hypocrite" negated. This suggests that it is possible for a person simply to act out love ("hypocrisy" originally meant "playing a part"). Calvin had stern words for any pretense in love: "It is difficult to express how ingenious almost all men are in counterfeiting a love which they do not really possess. . . . They persuade themselves that they have a true love for those whom they not only treat with neglect, but also in fact reject." True Christian love is without pretense or hypocrisy. It is absolutely genuine.

2. "Hate what is evil; cling to what is good" (12:9). We take these two statements together because of the obvious contrast. *Weymouth* translates, "Regard evil with horror." The Christian's best defense against wickedness is never to get over being shocked by it. This has become especially difficult in twentieth-century America where television is dominated by so much that is crude and vulgar. It is all too easy to grow comfortable surrounded by evil. Paul's admonition is to abhor it!

Cling rather to what is good. In early Greek the verb meant "to glue together." Fix yourself firmly to those things which are good and right. Paul exhorted the Philippians to think about that which was true, noble, right, pure, lovely, admirable, excellent and praiseworthy (see Phil. 4:8). By hating the evil and clinging to the good, God's purposes for His people are advanced.

3. "Be devoted to one another in brotherly love" (Rom 12:10). There must exist between the members of the Christian community a bond of tender affection. Believers are to care for one another as brothers in a closely-knit family. The Greek word for "brotherly love" is *philadelphia*. The ancient city of Philadelphia (in Asia Minor, see Rev. 3:7-13) was so named in honor of Attalus II who relinquished his crown to his older brother Eumenes II upon learning that the report of his assassination was only a rumor. This attitude earned him the name of Philadel-

phus (lover of his brother). The strength of this relationship has been undermined in modern times due to the gradual disintegration of the family unit. Many people consider "brotherly love" an ironic term; if not that, then certainly a broad term for general goodwill to others. As used by Paul the word is a much stronger and more virile expression. It involves commitment, fidelity and tender affection.

4. "Honor one another above yourselves" (Rom. 12:10). Interpreters have puzzled over this admonition. A literal translation would be, "In honor one another preferring." Philippians 2:3 encourages a similar attitude: "In humility consider others better than yourselves."

Paul is not asking each Christian to pretend that he is inferior to everyone else he meets. Spirituality does not require that we continually let others know how unimportant we are! What Paul asks is that we consider others worthy of preferential treatment. We are to put the welfare of others ahead of our own. We honor others not by empty praise but by giving them top priority. As Jesus said, "The greatest among you will be your servant. For whoever exalts himself [the direct opposite of Paul's admonition] will be humbled, and whoever humbles himself [read 'in honor preferring one another'] will be exalted" (Matt. 23:11,12).

Karl Barth has a keen insight at this point. It is as the other person that Christ mysteriously comes to me; He comes as the one who is hungry and thirsty, a stranger or a prisoner. By responding to those in need we honor Him (see Matt. 25:34-40). It is His presence in the one in need that explains why we are to honor others above ourselves.

5. "Never be lacking in zeal" (Rom 12:11). The new life in Christ Jesus allows no place for laziness. It calls for an intensity appropriate to the urgency of the issues in-

volved. When the one-talent servant reported his failure to get a return on his master's investment, he was severely reprimanded as a "wicked, lazy [same Greek word as "lacking in zeal"] servant" (Matt. 25:26).

We live in troubled times. The international picture is one of turmoil and unrest. The major world powers have at their disposal more than enough destructive power to remove from the face of our planet the entire civilization of mankind. The church holds the only answer to the human predicament. Now is not the time to sit idly by while the world hastens toward self-destruction. Christians are to be about their ministry of reconciliation with diligence and zeal.

6. "Keep your spiritual fervor" (Rom. 12:11). The *RSV* translates, "Be aglow with the Spirit," that is, the Holy Spirit. Our "spiritual life" is simply the presence and life of God's Spirit within us. We are to allow ourselves to be set on fire by the Spirit. The word "burning" was commonly used of boiling water or other liquids. Occasionally it was used of solids in which case it described them as fiery hot or glowing. The second usage is more appropriate here. We are to allow God's Spirit to burn within us and keep us glowing.

The church at Laodicea had disregarded such counsel (see Rev. 3:14-18). The fires of devotion had gradually lost their warmth and lukewarmness had settled in. Jesus says to the lukewarm, "Because you are . . . neither hot nor cold—I am about to spit you out of my mouth" (Rev. 3:16). There is no place in the church for those who have lost what Origen (in the third century) called "the fire of faith." Barclay notes that "the Christian may burn out, but he must not rust out." Paul's words in 1 Thessalonians 5:19 are relevant: "Do not put out the Spirit's fire." Our job is not to stir ourselves into a blaze but rather to allow the Spirit's fire to maintain in our lives a spiritual glow.

7. "Serve the Lord." Rather than "Lord" (*kurios*) some manuscripts have "time" (*kairos*). Since scribes often used abbreviations it is easy to understand how this confusion might arise (the contraction in each case would be *krs*). If the second reading is followed, Paul would be saying, "Seize the opportunities as they come." Although this is sound advice it is probably not what Paul intended.

It is likely that the admonition to be "aglow with the Spirit" would lead some members of the church to conclude that Paul placed an extremely high premium on the more exciting aspects of the Christian life. In every congregation there are those who display this tendency. So Paul immediately adds, "Be true bondsmen of your Lord" (*Conybeare*). You are called to serve as one who lives under the authority of a heavenly Master. Be aglow with the Spirit? Certainly! But remember that your calling is to carry out in practical daily life the will of the Lord.

8. "Be joyful in hope" (v. 12). *Moffatt* has, "Let your hope be joy to you." The source of Christian joy is the hope (the certainty of that which will surely come to pass) which will find its fulfillment when Christ returns, the righteous are vindicated and God establishes His eternal reign. Romans 5:2 said that "we rejoice in the hope of the glory of God." We joyfully anticipate the day when we will regain the glorious place which was forfeited by the sin of Adam.

The place of joy in the Christian life needs to be underscored repeatedly. God is a God of joy. The prophet Zephaniah exults, "The Lord your God is with you. . . . He will take great delight in you, . . . he will rejoice over you with singing" (Zeph. 3:17). The angel of the Lord announced to the shepherds the birth of Jesus, saying, "I bring you good news of great joy" (Luke 2:10). Joy, says

Paul, is a "fruit of the Spirit" (Gal. 5:22). Thus God in all three of His persons is a God of joy. As we His children await the final outcome of history we rejoice in our hope.

9. "Patient in affliction." It is necessary to be steadfast in times of trouble because opposition is the natural reaction of the world to the church. One of the last things Jesus told His band of disciples was, "In this world you will have trouble" (John 16:33). And that is exactly what happened. Toward the end of his first missionary journey Paul retraced his steps through the towns where he had recently ministered (and been mistreated—in Lystra he was stoned and left for dead). He strengthened the disciples and encouraged them to remain true to the faith saying, "We must go through many hardships to enter the kingdom of God" (Acts 14:22). Remaining patient under stress is a characteristic Christian virtue.

10. "Faithful in prayer." It is instructive that the word on prayer follows the warning about affliction. Prayer helps us to see behind the problem of the moment and discern the hand of God in every adverse situation. Prayer is not release from difficulty but a drawing upon divine strength to allow adversity to fulfill its purpose in our life. Prayer is tapping the strength of God for help in our weakness. Our greatest need—not only in times of trial but throughout life—is to "steadfastly maintain the habit of prayer" (*Phillips*). If you wonder why the church is so often weak and ineffectual, note that it is more often on its feet than on its knees; and this in spite of the fact that the Lord of the church said, "Apart from me you can do nothing" (John 15:5).

11. "Share with God's people who are in need" (v. 13). Someone said that the true measure of a man is demonstrated by his relationship to those less fortunate than himself. The essence of love is giving. The person

who bends every effort to secure his own position in the world is not motivated by Christian love. A nation (like America) which annually spends more for cat food than for foreign missions can hardly be called Christian. The practical nature of New Testament ethics calls for action wherever need exists. Certainly God's people in need represent a primary responsibility.

12. "Practice hospitality." The *NIV* misses the thrust of the admonition. "Practice" is a weak translation of the Greek verb "to pursue." Christian hospitality is more than bringing in the stranger at the door. It involves going out and actively pursuing those who would benefit from our kindness and concern. The participle is present tense suggesting that we make it our regular practice. Believers are not to withdraw from the society in which they live; rather they are to display in practical ways the care of God for every man in need.

For Discussion

This chapter provides many areas for profitable discussion. One is the role of the Christian in his relationship to the surrounding culture. It is easy to say that we are in the world but not of it, but what exactly does that mean? What does it mean in 12:2 not to be conformed to the pattern of this world? What is the world? Should we stand out against it? Aren't we to communicate the message of God to this world? How can we if we are so different that no one will listen? Do you think that non-Christians like to see us look and act like them? How does being transformed by the renewing of the inner man affect our relationship to this world? We are sometimes urged to be as much like the non-Christian as possible. Can this be supported from Scripture?

11

The Obligations of Love

Romans 13

Chapter 13 of Romans consists of three rather clearly defined sections. Verses 1-7 discuss the proper relationship between the Christian and the state. Verses 8-10 set forth the obligations of love, and verses 11-14 stress the urgency of the hour in view of the soon return of Christ. While the relationship between the second and third sections is quite clear, many commentators believe that the first unit is a parenthesis, independent of the context and inserted by Paul for reasons of his own. Kasemann calls it "an alien body in Paul's exhortation."

There is, however, a clear train of thought that ties together the entire chapter and connects it to its larger context. In the preceding chapter Paul has spoken of the Christians' relationship with one another (see 12:9-13) and with those outside the church (see 12:14-21). In the following chapter, 14, he will discuss at length the relationship between the stronger and the weaker brother. It would be surprising if in such an extended exhortation (12:1—15:13) he would not touch on such an important subject as the relationship between the Christian and the governing authorities. You will remember that a major problem for the early church—one that lasted until the edict of toleration in A.D. 312—was the hostility of the Roman Empire towards Christianity.

The central theme of chapter 13 is the obligation imposed by love. "Let no debt remain," writes Paul, ". . . except the continuing debt to love one another" (13:8). Obedience to the state (see vv. 1-7) should be seen as one of the obligations of love. The obligation to love one's fellowman (and thus fulfill the law) is especially urgent because the night is nearly over and the endless day of eternity is dawning (see vv. 11-14). This natural train of thought binds chapter 13 together and helps us to understand each segment in its proper contextual relationship.

"Submitting" to the State

Romans 13:1-7 is the classic presentation of the believers' obligation to governing authorities. Other New Testament writers treat the subject as well. Peter, for example, says, "Submit yourselves for the Lord's sake to every authority instituted among men" (1 Pet. 2:13). In later centuries the church fathers also spoke to the issue. Tertullian (third century) says that a Christian is to look up to the emperor because he "is called by our Lord to his office."

The immediate problem with this first section is that it seems to counsel absolute obedience to the state without regard to whether it is benign or wicked. Paul says, "There is no authority except that which God has established" (v. 1). To rebel against the existing authority is to rebel against God (see v. 2). Rulers are the servants of God and authorized to punish "the wrongdoer" (v. 4). They are due proper respect and honor (see v. 7).

All this sounds well and good in the ideal society. But history demonstrates with regularity that the wrong people frequently become the governing authorities. In Paul's day it was a crazed Nero who set fire to Rome and laid the blame on Christians. In our own day we think of the Third

Reich whose Führer ordered the mass execution of six million Jews and an even larger number of Christians! Recent slaughters in Africa and the Near East are vivid reminders of the devastation and cruelty that accompany unrestrained power. How can the Christian submit to such leadership? How can it be said that such authorities are servants of God to do His will?

One approach is to cite all the advantages of good government. The state preserves order and protects the citizen from harm. Without the state, chaos would reign. The state provides for the citizen a wide range of services (water, power, transportation, etc.) which could not exist at the same level through other agencies. But all this assumes a good government. The problem of the evil abuse of power continues. What should the Christian living under an oppressive and wicked regime do when ordered to take an action that runs counter to Christian convictions? Is Paul encouraging blind obedience to *all* governments in *every* situation?

Another approach is to stress that any specific statement in Scripture is qualified by all of Scripture. For instance, Jesus said, "If you believe, you will receive whatever you ask for in prayer" (Matt. 21:22). Yet we know that Jesus' "whatever" is limited to those things which are in accord with His will and conform to His character (that is, they can be asked for "in his name"). Therefore when Romans 13:1-7 counsels submission to the authority of government we naturally supply the qualification that such authority be carried out in a proper fashion. Otherwise submission is not binding. Even Jesus disobeyed when He refused to answer the questions of Herod or perform a miracle for his amusement (see Luke 23:8,9). And Peter and John boldly declared to the hostile Sanhedrin, "Judge for yourselves whether it is right in

God's sight to obey you rather than God. For we cannot help speaking about what we have seen and heard" (Acts 4:19,20).

So there is biblical precedent for *not* obeying the governing authorities when their demands run counter to our understanding of God's will and what is morally right. The war crime trials at Nuremberg show that in contemporary jurisprudence it is, under certain circumstances, wrong to obey the demands of the state.

The problem of submission to authority is alleviated somewhat when we examine more closely the key word in verse 1. The Greek word *hupotassesthai* (30 times in the New Testament) does not have *as its predominant thought* the idea of obedience. As used in Ephesians 5:21 ("Submit to one another"), it involves a reciprocal obligation. It is clear that husband and wife cannot always obey each other. Whenever their desires differ, one must submit to the other or some compromise be worked out. In either case the idea of unqualified obedience on a reciprocal basis is not observed. It can't be! The Greek verb as used in the New Testament denotes the conduct which flows naturally from the recognition that the other person comes as Christ's representative and therefore has an infinitely greater claim upon us than we have upon ourselves. Cranfield (who discusses this point at length) concludes that Paul is speaking of an authoritarian state in which Christian obedience is limited to respecting the authorities, obeying them when such obedience does not conflict with God's laws, paying taxes willingly, and praying persistently for them (see 1 Tim. 2:1,2).

With this understanding of "submission" in mind, we can learn from verses 1-7 the origin of government and its role in God's plan for the welfare of man. The existing authorities have been established by God, verse 1. To rebel against authority is to rebel against what God has instituted, verse 2. Those who carry out the functions of government are servants of God and entrusted with the power of the sword to bring about justice and punish the wrongdoer, verse 4. Respect for government as a divinely initiated method to prevent social chaos and obedience to its requirements (when they don't run counter to God's laws) are among the major obligations of love. It is this underlying thought that provides continuity with that which follows.

The Ultimate Obligation

Paul has just listed several obligations of the Christian to the governing authorities. "If you owe taxes, pay taxes; if revenue, then revenue; if respect, then respect; if honor, then honor" (v. 7). He continues, "Leave no debt unpaid except the standing debt of mutual love" (v. 8, *Weymouth*). The debt of love, unlike other debts, requires constant payment, yet can never be paid up. Many years ago Origen (a third-century Christian theologian) wrote, "It is expedient that we should both pay this debt daily and always owe it." It is the ultimate obligation, the unlimited responsibility of all who have been touched by the saving power of God.

Love is the consummate moral responsibility in that it fulfills everything required by the law (see vv. 8,10). What Paul is saying is that when a person genuinely strives to discharge the debt of love, he will automatically keep the commandments. For example, sincere love for another will preclude adultery. It is impossible to care for another person and disregard God's will regarding extra-marital relationships. Love for the other person makes murder impossible. It makes stealing and coveting out of the question. Love establishes a relationship in which all

of the commandments of the second table of the Deca-
logue are unnecessary. To love is to bring to completion
the deepest intent of the Old Testament moral legislation.
Love fulfills the law.

The relationship between love and law becomes clear-
er when we understand law in terms of its intention. The
laws of God are not the whims of a capricious deity. They
do not exist as a basis for punishment. They are expressions of the will of God and therefore good and gracious.
The article in Kittel's well-known *Theological Dictionary
of the New Testament* says that the law is "the divine gift
which will show the people what conduct accords with its
position as God's own people . . . [It] is thus a demonstration of grace." As an expression of the divine will, law
reflects the nature of God Himself. How gracious of God
that He should tell us what He is like lest we unknowingly
act contrary to His character!

Love fulfills the law because in the final analysis law
is the expression of love in the complexities of a fallen
world. The purpose of the law has been to sketch out how
love conducts itself in the details of life. It is by nature
temporary. With Christ as our model (the fullest expression of the nature of God), we no longer need to concen-
trate on the written codes of antiquity. We turn rather to
Christ as the living example of what it means to love
others.

There is an important point in verse 8 which often
slips by unnoticed. The *NIV* has, "For he who loves his
fellow man has fulfilled the law." The impression is left
that it is sufficient to love others (in a general sense). But
the Greek text has a definite article and reads "the other";
the love which fulfills the law is a love that goes out to the
specific person who at that particular moment confronts
us in need. He is *the other* who is brought across our path

by God and therefore has a claim on our service. Cranfield notes that, "the 'neighbor' in the New Testament sense is not someone arbitrarily chosen by us: he is given to us by God."

The requirement to love one's neighbor (in this sense) is clear from the parable of the good Samaritan. The scholar asked, "And who is my neighbor?" (Luke 10:29). By the end of the parable he had his answer. The priest and the Levite tried to circumvent need but the Samaritan responded with concern and loving care (see Luke 10:30-37). Every person in need whom God brings to our attention is our "neighbor." Our response to need indicates whether or not we are fulfilling the law by loving *the other*. Unfortunately, it is easier to "love" others as an abstract group than it is to love a specific individual who right now desires and needs the assistance I am able to give.

At the great judgment of the sheep and the goats in Matthew 25:31-46, those who will inherit the kingdom will be the ones who have actually responded to such lowly needs of others as food, shelter, hospitality, clothes, and companionship (see vv. 35,36). In a related context John says, "If anyone has material possessions and sees his brother in need but has no pity on him, how can the love of God be in him?" (1 John 3:17). And James puts it bluntly, "Suppose a brother or sister is without clothes and daily food. If one of you says to him, 'Go, I wish you well; keep warm and well fed,' but does nothing about his physical needs, what good is it?" (Jas. 2:15,16).

Love which is not translated into acts of love is not love. In fact, a good case can be made for the proposition that love exists only in actual deeds of love. Abstractions are convenient for philosophical discourse but are without substance and have no value for those in need. We are to love *the other*, the neighbor who is there—whose need has a claim on our time and energy because God brought him across our path at a particular moment in time.

The continuing debt of love is the obligation of grace. While justification does not depend upon ethical performance it must *necessarily* result in an entirely new relationship to God, to ourselves, and to others. It is the grand reversal. Love of self has been transposed into love of God and all for whom Christ died. The believer's perspective on all the vital issues of life has undergone a radical transformation. In another place Paul exclaims, "Therefore, if anyone is in Christ, he is a new creation; the old has gone, the new has come!" (2 Cor. 5:17). Or, as *Phillips* puts it, "The past is finished and gone, everything has become fresh and new." To all who have committed themselves without reserve to meeting the needs of *the other*, life has in fact become "fresh and new."

The Day Is at Hand

The brevity of time is a theme that permeates the literature of man. Shelley speaks of "time's fleeting river," and Tennyson reminds us that "Time driveth onward fast." Isaac Watts in his great eighteenth-century hymn writes, "Time, like an ever-rolling stream, bears all its sons away; they fly forgotten, as a dream dies at the opening day." Mankind has always been painfully aware that time is always running out. It is the only irreplaceable commodity. Death marches relentlessly on without regard to the wealth or prestige of its victims.

The limited nature of each person's time on earth is what gives life both its urgency and its grandeur. For years Rollo May, widely known psychoanalyst, has taught that it is by accepting the limits of human mortality that people are set free to live. Paul brings another kind of limitation on time into the picture. In verse 12 he writes, "The night is nearly over; the day is almost here." The "night," of course, is the present age, and the "day" is the coming age of God's universal and eternal reign. It is specifically because mankind is living at the end of time that the necessity to love takes on heightened significance. The time for compassionate concern will not continue indefinitely. Opportunities for kindness are running out. This age of "darkness" is about over; the new and eternal age is dawning. We sing, "Work for the night is coming"—we should sing, "Love for the *day* is coming!"

Paul tells his readers, in verse 11, that they should understand "the present time." It is time to awaken from the drowsiness of ineffectual and slothful living. Why? "Because our salvation is nearer now than when we first believed." The salvation of which Paul speaks is that great deliverance which will take place at the return of Christ. He is not thinking of individual salvation at this point. An urgency exists because that great day when God's kingdom will be established in its complete and eternal form is almost upon us. Now is not the time to sleep. The first rays of the eternal day have appeared on the horizon of history.

The theme of the nearness of the end runs throughout the New Testament. Jesus told His followers that when they saw certain things happen they would know that the end would be "right at the door" (Mark 13:29). In one of his last letters Paul told the Philippians, "The Lord is near" (Phil. 4:5). And John said, "Dear children, this is the last hour" (1 John 2:18). Additional verses could be cited. The obvious problem is that 2,000 years have gone by and the end (which seemed to have been expected momentarily) has not yet come. If Scripture is wrong about an event of such importance, how can we have confidence in what it teaches about other things? Why, for instance, should we go to all the trouble of loving our neighbors when this too may be in error?

Many answers to this dilemma have been set forth. By far the most satisfactory approach is that which recognizes that the biblical writers were not thinking primarily in temporal terms. They were not studying the calendar and working out a specific timetable. A great realization had laid hold of them and conditioned their entire perspective: with the life, death, and resurrection of Jesus, the end time had already begun. From this point on nothing would be added which in any way could affect the finality of all that had been accomplished in and through Christ. Anything that took place from that point forward must be considered an epilogue. Of course Christ would come, but His coming would not require some new action upon which everything else depended. Victory over Satan was won on the cross; then followed the triumph of the resurrection which forever established the reign and rule of God. It is in this sense that the end is near. Whether or not the intervening period will last for x number of years is secondary. The coming of Christ is near because everything that needs to be done has been accomplished.

In view of the dawning day, believers are to "put aside the deeds of darkness" (those activities which belong to the dark nature of this evil world) and "put on the armor of light" (that is, the armor provided by God and drawing its strength from the coming day) (Rom. 13:12). Paul describes the armor in another place as the "belt of truth . . . the breastplate of righteousness . . . [the sandals] of peace . . . the shield of faith . . . the helmet of salvation and the sword of the Spirit" (Eph. 6:14-17). These qualities belong to the new age. They provide spiritual strength and protection to live out our remaining days until Christ returns.

Paul continues his night/day metaphor. "Let us behave decently, as in the daytime" (Rom. 13:13). Evil actions are regularly associated with the darkness of night. Jesus, reflecting on man's rejection of the light, said, "Men loved darkness instead of light because their deeds were evil" (John 3:19).

In Romans 13:13 Paul lists six deeds of darkness which are to be no part of the believer's life. That the first four are listed in the plural suggests frequent repetition. "Revellings and drunken bouts" (*Rotherham*) are closely linked. Although the Greeks were a wine-drinking people, they held drunkenness to be a particularly disgraceful condition. "Sexual immorality" was a widespread social sin throughout the ancient world. Fidelity to one's spouse was not held to be a virtue, and the result was extensive promiscuity. The word translated "debauchery" has been called "one of the ugliest words in the Greek language." It describes the person without shame. While many people try to cover over their wickedness, the "shameless man" is perfectly willing for the entire world to know the extent of his degradation.

The final pair are "quarrelling and jealousy" (*TCNT*). We tend to think of these sins as being more socially acceptable—but are they? Strife or contention is born out of the sinful desire to get ahead at any cost; it is the negation of love. Envy is the dark side of lovelessness; it expresses man's evil reaction to the good fortune of another.

Since strife and envy are linked with sexual immorality we ought to be reminded that God's standards do not always conform to our socially acceptable mores.

Instead of being caught up in the deeds of darkness, we are to "clothe [ourselves] with the Lord Jesus Christ" and "put a stop to gratifying the evil desires that lurk in

[our] lower nature" (v. 14, *Williams*). To put on Christ means to identify oneself totally and continually with everything He is. To put Him on is to embrace His person for our lives here and now. It is to so merge ourself in Him that He is the One who lives out His life through us. This kind of life automatically excludes the responses we might otherwise make to the promptings of our fallen nature. Paul holds out no hope that man's evil nature will somehow be removed. The tendency to act independently and contrary to the will of God will always remain. It does not remain, however, as a force that is unable to be controlled. Wherever our fallen nature asserts itself successfully, it is because we have allowed it to do so. Because we are indwelt by the Spirit of God, we are now empowered to resist its promptings and choose not to sin. We are able *not* "to gratify the desires of [our] sinful nature."

The two final verses of chapter 13 will always be famous in that they were used by God in the conversion of Augustine, the famous fifth-century church father to whom we owe so much in the development of Christian theology. In his *Confessions* he tells about lamenting his misspent youth and hearing a childlike voice saying, "Take and read." Turning to Scripture, his eyes fell on this passage and suddenly all became clear. The light of assurance flooded his experience. He closed the book and turning to a friend shared his life-changing experience.

For Discussion

At times it seems that those truths which lie closest to the heart of what it means to be a Christian are the very truths we understand the least. Take love for instance. When we read that love fulfills the law, what does that mean to us in a practical way? Are we still confused about the nature of love? Is love no more than a warm feeling for the other person? Does our "love" in any real way reflect the self-giving love of God as expressed once for all in the giving of His Son to die for our sins?

It is the nature of evil to make things mean the opposite. Has this happened with love? Think about the last few times you have heard the word on TV. Is that kind of love Christian concern in action? God has called us to love Him supremely and to love one another (see Matt. 22:34-40). Are we in fact loving in that way? Are God's greater honor and the welfare of others our major ethical concerns? Are we loving "the other"—the one in need whom God has brought across our path? Let us return to the basics and learn anew the great ethical imperatives of the Christian church. Are you with me?

12

Getting Along for the Glory of God

Romans 14:1—15:13

No matter who you are or where you live you'll always have to put up with two kinds of people—those who are more conservative than you and those who are more liberal. In every church there are those with freedom of conscience to do certain things which if you did would result in pangs of guilt. Then there are others who don't have the freedom to do what you are able to do with a perfectly free conscience.

When I was a boy we always went swimming on Sunday afternoon. It was great fun and I held my dad in high esteem for his "liberated" position at this point. Some friends, however, were not so lucky. Their parents honestly felt that Sunday was God's day in the sense that anything of a secular nature was inappropriate. We may think that not swimming on Sunday is an antiquated point of view—and perhaps it is—but we acknowledge the fact that the decision about it represents a principle that is as relevant today as it ever was.

The Stoics used to talk about certain things which they called *adiaphora*—that is, morally neutral, neither right nor wrong. All such things depend upon how a person views them. It is important to note that a great many things are always right (kindness, helpfulness, love) and a number of other things are always wrong (selfishness, cruelty, wastefulness). Scripture is not at all hesitant about pointing out the sinfulness of such things as sexual immorality, hatred, fits of rage and drunkenness (see Gal. 5:19,20). It is also perfectly clear that qualities such as love, patience, goodness and self-control are above reproach (see Gal. 5:22,23).

The difficulty arises not with those things expressly declared in Scripture to be right or wrong but with the *adiaphora,* all those practices which lie in between. Sometimes it is context or timing that raises doubt about an otherwise morally neutral act. Take a double-rich chocolate malt, for example. Is it good or bad? It is neither until you put it in context. To a ravenous teenager just in from several hours of strenuous physical activity it may well be good. To an overweight 40-year-old it is probably wrong. To the anchor man on a relay team (about to run) upon whom rests the outcome of his school's competition in an important track meet, it would be absolutely out of the question.

The final part of Paul's letter to the Romans deals with some first-century *adiaphora.* How should Christians in the same fellowship relate to one another in reference to these items? Paul writes, "One man's faith allows him to eat everything, but another man, whose faith is weak, eats only vegetables" (Rom. 14:2). You will remember that the Jewish people followed very strict dietary laws. Many foods were considered ceremonially unclean and should not be eaten. When people from this background became Christians they would quite naturally bring with them a certain abhorrence of unclean foods. Even though Jesus declared that a person cannot be made "unclean" by anything entering from without (see Mark 7:15), a lifetime of careful scruples made it too difficult for some to change their eating habits with a clear conscience.

Those who continued to feel an obligation to the ceremonial law, Paul calls the "weak" in faith. By contrast, the "strong" are those who can with a clear conscience grasp the fact that Christ is the fulfillment of the law and that, therefore, believers are no longer obliged to keep its ceremonial prescriptions.

These differences extended to other items such as the observance of certain days as sacred (see Rom. 14:5) and the eating of meat (see v. 6). Such things were by no means central to the Christian faith. Yet people felt strongly about them, and because of their potential to disrupt the unity of the church they receive extended discussion in Paul's letter.

We live today with the same basic problem. The specific issues have changed but the underlying problem is the same. In the local church certain believers allow themselves a freedom of conduct which is beyond what others may practice. (Remember, I'm not suggesting that *anything* goes if you can do it with a clear conscience. Scripture lays out rather clearly those activities which are off limits for the believer.) Other Christians operate rather narrowly and have chosen an extremely limited style of living. How to get along for the glory of God is Paul's major theme throughout this final section of his letter. His counsel needs attention in a day when the media have brought into our living rooms a level of "entertainment" which only a few years ago was considered the lowest form of burlesque.

Counsel for the "Weak"

Remember that the "weak" are not unstable or vacillating in regard to their faith in God. They are weak in the sense that they do not have the inner assurance that certain relatively unimportant things (e.g., eating with cere-

monially unwashed hands) are now permissible. Their
scruples keep them from enjoying a freedom in Christ
which is rightfully theirs. The natural tendency of the
weak Christian is to condemn the strong—the brother
who exercises greater freedom in what he does. So Paul
writes, "The man who does not eat everything must not
condemn the man who does" (14:3). Just because your
scruples keep you from eating meat which in former days
you considered as unclean (and you still can't believe it's
somehow okay) you have no right to judge another who
no longer shares your qualms. After all, God has accepted
your liberated brother (see v. 3), so, "Who are you to
judge someone else's servant? To his own master he
stands or falls" (v. 4). We will all stand before the judgment seat of God and each "will give account of *himself* to
God" (vv. 10-12, italics added). "Let us not . . . judge
one another" (v. 13, *KJV*).

A major temptation of the weak is to judge the conduct
of the strong. Someone defined carnality as that which
you do which I don't happen to do. God will judge the
actions of others. Our role is to consider prayerfully the
quality of our own life. The important thing for the weak
is that they do not violate their own conscience. Paul
himself is convinced that "no food is unclean in itself" (v.
14). The work of Christ has radically transformed the
ancient ritual laws of clean and unclean (see Mark 7:15;
Acts 10:14,28). Yet, "if anyone regards something as
unclean, then for him it is unclean" (Rom. 14:14). To eat
that which your conscience forbids is absolutely wrong.
"He is a fortunate man," declares Paul, "who has no
misgivings about what he allows himself to eat" (v. 22,
Moffatt). Obviously this is not a general statement
teaching the blessedness of an insensitive conscience. It is
rather a simple declaration that for one to live in accord-

ance with one's conscience brings happiness.

Paul goes on to say that "the man who has doubts is condemned if he eats, because his eating is not from faith; and everything that does not come from faith is sin" (v. 23). Or, as *Phillips* has it, "When we act apart from our faith [our conviction that what we are about to do is right in God's eyes] we sin." It is a serious matter to violate one's conscience. To do what we believe to be wrong is to undermine personal integrity. Without freedom of conscience we should take no further step. That others do a certain thing is beside the point. Paul teaches that if you feel a thing is wrong, then *for you it is wrong*. If you cannot act without misgivings, then for you it will be sin.

In summary, then, Paul counsels the weak to resist passing judgment on their Christian brothers who have the inner freedom to live apart from the ceremonial laws of Judaism, and secondly, not to violate their integrity by partaking in any practice which their conscience will not allow.

Counsel for the "Strong"

Paul spends more time with the strong than with the weak. Unity within the church depends more upon the attitude of the strong than upon a minority report from the weak. Paul opens the chapter by saying to the strong, "Accept him whose faith is weak" (14:1). Don't allow your own freedom in Christ to lead you to where you are unable to understand and accept your brethren who find it impossible to shake off the feeling that former restrictions may still be in force. Don't let your "enlightenment" make you judgmental or feel superior. Paul tells the strong not to pass "judgment on disputable matters" (v. 1) or to look down on those who eat "only vegetables" (vv. 2,3).

The strong should accept the weak for the same reason that the weak should not judge the strong—"Each of us will give an account of himself to God" (v. 12). There is to be no passing of judgment on the other (see vv. 3,10,13). In "disputable matters" (v. 1) the believing community is to live in love and exercise appropriate tolerance. Nothing is gained by a censorious attitude toward those whose faith has not allowed them to disregard certain taboos.

The primary obligation of the strong is never to do anything which would cause a brother to stumble or fall (see v. 13). Apparently the problem had already surfaced in the church at Rome. *Moffatt* has, "So let us stop criticizing one another." Carping criticism is the opposite of love. Instead of helping the situation it makes matters worse. It does not stem from an honest concern to encourage the growth of Christian character in the other person. More often than not criticism intends only to lower the person in the eyes of others while promoting one's own reputation. While often accomplishing the first it rarely achieves the second. We instinctively mistrust one who delights in running down others.

Instead of passing judgment we should resolve never to do anything which would cause our brother to stumble. This is Paul's central message to the strong. Do not "trip up or entangle a brother's conscience" (v. 13, *Knox*) by exercising the freedom your conscience allows. Love, not freedom, is the rule of Christian conduct. What we do must always be considered in the light of its effect on others. Even that which a person may hold to be morally neutral and acceptable before God must be set aside if it leads others to act against their conscience and so undermine their personal sense of right and wrong.

Beginning with verse 14 Paul shows how this principle works out in daily life. Paul himself is fully convinced that no food is intrinsically unclean. That's what Jesus declared in Mark 7:15. The ceremonial laws of the Old Testament are no longer in force. What was previously disallowed is now acceptable. However, "if anyone regards something as unclean, then for him it is unclean" (Rom. 14:14). We acknowledge a certain degree of moral relativity. Paul is not saying that anything is right as long as you think it is. That would lead to ethical chaos. He is saying that if a person does not have the inner freedom to accept something as morally neutral, then if he goes ahead against his conscience, it becomes wrong for him. The wrong consists not in the act as a hypothetical possibility but in the doing of something which one still feels is wrong. It is the violation of conscience which is wrong— the activity merely provides the opportunity for decision.

So, "if your brother is distressed because of what you eat, you are no longer acting in love" (v. 15). Your life is not being governed by love "if your habit of unrestricted diet seriously upsets your brother" (*Phillips*). It is a grave matter to bring ruin upon a brother for whom Christ died (v. 15). Your willful insistence upon "Christian freedom" may well mean disaster to your weaker brother, the very one for whom Christ died. Do you really want to be found working against the purposes of God? Insist on your "rights" and you'll find yourself in that very place.

The basic issue is crucial. Paul repeats himself in verses 20 and 21. Don't destroy the work of God simply for the sake of eating meat that you know to be ceremonially unclean. It is wrong for you "to eat anything that causes someone else to stumble" (v. 20). Because of its impact on others it is no longer a morally neutral option for you. Because it hurts the weaker brother it has become wrong for you. The right course of action is to give up eating meat and drinking wine or doing "anything else that will cause your brother to fall" (v. 21).

This basic principle is easier to handle as an abstract formulation than it is to put into practice in the concrete realities of daily life. Some attempt needs to be made to recast the principle into a twentieth-century setting. We don't live with "ceremonially unclean" foods today. We do face, however, a number of different modern practices about which the church universal holds varying opinions. They run the gamut from entertainment such as the cinema and punk rock all the way to abortion and military intervention. Christians are divided upon what sort of a stance is consistent with biblical revelation as it relates to these issues. How does Paul's teaching inform the attitude of the modern believer in regard to the "weaker" and the "stronger" brother?

It needs to be said once again that many things clearly fall outside that which Scripture allows. Our discussion here treats only the *adiaphora*. We have already seen that the believer (the "weaker" brother) who is unable with a clear conscience to take part in a certain activity is not to condemn the person who does. God did not intend that we sit as a jury pronouncing final judgment upon one another (see vv. 4,10). We also know that if the weaker brother engages in something about which he has doubts he condemns himself (vv. 22,23).

Most of the instruction in 14:1—15:13 is directed towards the "stronger" believer. Whatever your conviction on disputed matters, "Keep [it] between yourself and God" (v. 22). Don't make a public issue out of private concerns. You are under no mandate to set the world straight on secondary matters. The less said the better.

The first verses of chapter 15 highlight several responsibilities of the strong. First, "It is the duty of us who are strong to put up with the weaknesses of those who are immature" (v. 1, *Goodspeed*). Love requires patience and understanding. Since the weaker brother is in fact a Christian brother we are to extend to him a gentle compassion and understanding.

Secondly, we are "not to insist on having our own way" (v. 1, *Knox*). An overweening concern to have it our way is antithetical to love. Our lives are to be governed by the needs and welfare of others, not by an intense desire to focus in on what's in it for me. In this context "our way" is by no means *God's* way.

Thirdly, "Everyone of us must try to please his neighbor, to do him good, and help in his development" (v. 2, *Goodspeed*). Our lives should serve the best interests of the other person. This is what it means to love one another (the two commandments to love God and others summarize the entire ethical content of the Law and the Prophets; see Matt. 22:34-40). We need to build up the faith of one another, to help each other grow toward Christian maturity. These goals cannot be reached if we go through life insisting upon "Christian freedom" as a rule of conduct. Obviously we are free to live within the bounds of a conscience informed by scriptural revelation. Yet that very revelation now tells us that we are to restrict that freedom out of love for the weaker brother. It is love, not freedom, which serves as a guide for Christian conduct.

Some Parting Advice for Everyone

Paul now addresses both the weak and the strong. May God "give you a spirit of unity among yourselves as you follow Christ Jesus" (15:5). It is God's will that unity prevail in every congregation of believers. And it will prevail if we "follow Christ" who, according to 15:3, "did not please himself" but bore the insults of man's hostility toward God. If He was willing to go that far in not pleasing Himself we should be willing to lay aside our personal preferences and have patience with one another.

The purpose of unity is that we "may unite in a chorus of praise and glory" to the God and Father of our Lord Jesus Christ (v. 6, *Moffatt*). If everyone is insisting upon his rights, regardless of how it affects others, there will be no chorus of united praise to God.

Paul continues, "Accept one another, then, just as Christ accepted you" (15:7). Remember that you were welcomed into the family of God when you turned in faith to Him. You brought along all the baggage of past prejudices. Only now are you being molded into the person God wants you to be. Since God accepted you—warts and all—you should also accept others, even those who name the name of Christ but understand the implications of faith somewhat differently. Acceptance itself is intended "to bring praise to God" (v. 7).

Finally, both the weak and the strong are to be filled "with great joy and peace" in order that they may all "overflow with hope by the power of the Holy Spirit" (v. 13). This is Paul's deepest desire for the believers at Rome. *Phillips* captures Paul's idea with a remarkably apt translation of this final verse. The ultimate purpose of being filled with joy and peace is that "your whole life and outlook may be radiant with hope." The follower of Christ is not the person obsessed with the desire to discover what he can get by with and still be a Christian (the limits of his "freedom"). He is the one who lays aside personal prerogatives if they in any way hurt his fellow believer and reaches out for the peace and joy which come from a life of obedience to the spirit of his Master. It is commitment to Christ (not to personal advantage) that results in a life that is "radiant with hope."

For Discussion

From a practical standpoint, this section of Romans is

of great importance to the life of the church. The principle is relatively easy to understand; the application is more difficult. As a group, pick out several contemporary issues where there will be a difference of opinion. The purpose of the exercise is not to convince others of the correctness of your point of view. Rather, show how you are to live in relationship to those who exercise greater freedom (the stronger) or less freedom (the weaker) on the issue. You will undoubtedly find that in your group there will be those on both sides.

For a starter let me mention several issues where Christians differ. What about wine? Paul brought it up in 14:21. How about the cinema? Are G and GP okay but R and X off limits? What about the believer who goes to R-rated movies in order to understand how the secular world understands life? Or what about the Christian who limits himself to Disney movies? Do you feel superior and better informed? Do you show this attitude? If so, what is the impact on your fellow believer?

Follow this procedure through on a number of issues. Remember, you are not to argue the point or try to convince those who see it differently (that can be done in a different forum). Here the purpose is to examine whether our own relationships to the weaker and stronger brethren reflect Paul's teaching in this section of Romans.

Bibliography

Barclay, William. *The Letter to the Romans,* The Daily Study Bible. Philadelphia: Westminster Press.

Barrett, Charles K. *Epistle to the Romans*. New York: Harper & Row Publishers, 1958.

Barth, Karl. *Epistle to the Romans*. New York: Oxford University Press, 1968.

Black, Matthew. *Romans,* New Century Bible Series. Greenwood, SC: Attic Press, 1973.

Blamires, Harry. *The Christian Mind*. Ann Arbor, MI: Servant Publications, 1978.

Bruce, F.F. *The Epistle of Paul to the Romans,* Tyndale Bible Commentaries. Wheaton, IL: Tyndale House Publishers, 1963.

Calvin, John. *The Epistles to the Romans and to the Thessalonians,* Calvin's New Testament Commentaries. Grand Rapids: Wm. B. Eerdmans Publishing Co., nd.

Cranfield, Charles E. *Epistle to the Romans,* International Critical Commentary Series. Naperville, IL: Alec R. Allenson, Inc., vol. 1, 1975; vol. 2, 1979.

Dodd, C.H. *The Epistle of Paul to the Romans,* Moffatt New Testament Commentary. London: Hodder and Stoughton, 1932.

Hunter, A.M. *The Epistle to the Romans,* Torch Bible

Commentaries. Naperville, IL: Alec R. Allenson, Inc., 1955.

———— *Introducing New Testament Theology*. Philadelphia: Westminster Press, 1958.

Kasemann, Ernst. *Commentary on Romans*. Grand Rapids: Wm. B. Eerdmans Publishing Co., 1978.

Kittel, Gerhard. *Theological Dictionary of the New Testament* (10 vols.). Grand Rapids: Wm. B. Eerdmans Publishing Co., 1964-1976.

Laubach, Frank. *Prayer, the Mightiest Force in the World*. Old Tappan, NJ: Fleming H. Revell Co., nd.

Murray, John. *The Epistle of Paul to the Romans*, New International Commentary on the New Testament. Grand Rapids: Wm. B. Eerdmans Publishing Co., 1960.

Nygren, A. *Commentary on Romans*. Philadelphia: Fortress Press, 1949.

Sagan, Carl. *Cosmos (New York: Random House, Inc., 1981)*.

Sanday, William and Headlam, Arthur C., *Romans*. Naperville, IL: Alec R. Allenson, Inc., 1902.

Taylor, Vincent. *The Epistle to the Romans*, Epworth Preacher's Commentary. London, 1956.